TOYS
IN THE ATTIC

BY LILLIAN HELLMAN

★

★

DRAMATISTS
PLAY SERVICE
INC.

Hudson Theatre. Premier performance February 25, 1960. Kermit Bloomgarden presents Jason Robards, Jr., Maureen Stapleton and Irene Worth in Lillian Hellman's new play TOYS IN THE ATTIC, with Anne Revere, Rochelle Oliver, Percy Rodriguez. Directed by Arthur Penn. Setting and lighting by Howard Bay. Costumes by Ruth Morley.

CAST
(*In Order of Appearance.*)

CARRIE BERNIERS................*Maureen Stapleton*
ANNA BERNIERS.....................*Anne Revere*
GUS ....*Charles McRae*
ALBERTINE PRINE....................*Irene Worth*
HENRY SIMPSON...................*Percy Rodriguez*
JULIAN BERNIERS................*Jason Robards, Jr.*
LILY BERNIERS.....................*Rochelle Oliver*
TAXI DRIVER......................*William Hawley*
THREE MOVING MEN,
       Clifford Cothren, Tom Manley, Maurice Ellis

"French Lessons in Songs" and "Bernier Day" by
MARC BLITZSTEIN

Production Stage Manager
KERMIT KEGLEY

PLACE: The Berniers house in New Orleans.

ACT ONE
Six P. M. on a summer Tuesday.

ACT TWO
Eight A. M. the following morning.

ACT THREE
Shortly after.

3

Toys in the Attic

ACT ONE

PLACE: *The* BERNIERS *living room, entrance-porch to the house, and small city-garden off the porch. The house is solid middle-class of another generation. The furniture is heavy and old. Everything inside and outside is neat, but in need of repairs. The porch has a rocking chair and is crowded with plants. The garden has a stool* D. L., *a low table* C., *and a bench* R. *that have been painted too often and don't stay together very well. It is a house lived in by poor, clean, orderly people who don't like where they live.*

AT RISE: ANNA BERNIERS, *carrying her gloves and purse and still wearing her hat, pushes open the blinds of the windows that give on the garden. She lifts a large camellia pot and puts it outside. She pours a glass of water on the plant and moves back into the room to take off her hat.* ANNA *is a nice-looking woman, calm and quiet. She is about forty-two.* CARRIE BERNIERS *appears from the street, climbs the porch steps. She is about thirty-eight, still pretty, but the prettiness is wearing thin and tired. She fans herself, rocks back and forth, the chair creaks and sways and, wearily, she rises and moves to trash basket to throw tissue away.*

CARRIE. (*As she hears* ANNA *enter from kitchen.*) That you, Anna?
ANNA. (*Crosses to* U. L. *sideboard, gets apron and starts to put it on.*) Just got home.
CARRIE. Hot. (*Sits on porch rocker.*)
ANNA. Paper says a storm.
CARRIE. I know. I'll take the plants in.

5

ANNA. I just put them out. Let them have a little storm air.

CARRIE. I don't like them out in a storm. Worries me. I don't like storms. I don't believe plants do, either.

ANNA. (*Gets pair of slippers from off* U. L., *returns to living room and sits chair* D. L.; *speaks out toward the porch.*) Did you have a hard day?

CARRIE. He let me leave the office after lunch. "You're looking a little peaked, Miss Berniers, from the heat." I said I've been looking a little peaked for years in heat, in cold, in rain, when I was young, and now. You mean *you're* hot and want to go home, you faker, I said. Only I said it to myself.

ANNA. (*Changes shoes.*) We had a private sale at the store. Coats. Coats on a day like this. There was a very good bargain, red with black braid. I had my eye on it for you all last winter. But—

CARRIE. Oh, I don't need a coat.

ANNA. (*Rises and exits with shoes* U. L.) Yes, you do. Did you go to the park? I wanted to, but the sale went so late. Old lady Senlis and old lady Condelet just sat there, looking at everything, even small coats. (*Re-enters.*) How can rich people go to a sale on a day like this?

CARRIE. I feel sorry for them. For all old ladies. Even rich ones. Money makes them lonely.

ANNA. (*Gets two glasses* U. L.) Why would that be?

CARRIE. Don't you feel sorry for old ladies? You used to.

ANNA. (*Crosses and puts glasses table* C.) When my feet don't hurt and I don't have to sell them coats at a sale. Was it nice in the park?

CARRIE. I didn't go to the park. I went to the cemetery.

ANNA. (*Sighs and exits* D. L.) Everybody still there?

CARRIE. I took flowers. It's cool there. Cooler. I was the only person there. Nobody goes to see anybody in summer. Yet those who have passed away must be just as lonely in summer as they are in winter. Sometimes I think we shouldn't have put Mama and Papa at Mount Olive Cemetery. (ANNA *re-enters with plate of ice and*

6

pitcher of tea.) Maybe it would have been nicer for them at Mount Great Hope with the new rich people. What would you think if we don't get buried at Mount Olive with Mama and Papa?

ANNA. (*Leaves tea things on* C. *table.*) Any place that's cool. (*Gets scissors* U. L. *and crosses to porch.*)

CARRIE. I bought you a small bottle of Eau D'haut Alpine. Cologne water of the high Alps, I guess. (*Holds up a package.*) Your weekly present. What did you buy me, may I ask, who shouldn't?

ANNA. Jar of candied oranges. (*Crosses* D. R. *to yard and cuts mint.*)

CARRIE. Oh, how nice. We'll have them for a savory. Do you know I read in our travel book on England that *they* think a proper savory is an anchovy. Anchovy after dinner. They won't make me eat it. What are you doing?

ANNA. Nothing. I'm going to clean. (*Comes back in, puts scissors on* U. L. *sideboard.*)

CARRIE. Oh, don't. Sunday's cleaning day. Was this house always so big?

ANNA. (*Crosses to* C. *table, pours tea.*) It grew as people left it.

CARRIE. I want to tell you something I've never told you before. I never, ever, liked this house. Not even when we were children. I know *you* did, but I didn't.

ANNA. (*Puts mint in tea.*) You know I liked it?

CARRIE. I don't think Julian ever liked it, either. That's why we used to have our supper out here on the steps. Did you ever know that's why I used to bring Julian out here, even when he was a baby, and we'd have our supper on the steps? I didn't want him to find out about the house. Julian and I. Nice of Mama and Papa to let us, wasn't it? Must have been a great deal of trouble carrying the dishes out here. Mama had an agreeable nature.

ANNA. (*Gives* CARRIE *a glass of tea.*) I carried the dishes out. (*Crosses back to* C. *table in parlor.*)

CARRIE. Did you? Yes, so you did. Thank you, Anna. Thank you very much. Did you mind eating with Mama and Papa (*Points off.*) in that awful oak tomb?

ANNA. Yes, I minded.

7

CARRIE. Well, it sure was a nice thing to do. I never knew you minded. Funny how you can live so close and long and not know things, isn't it?

ANNA. (*Sits R. chair, sips tea.*) Yes, indeed. I called Mr. Shine today. He said he hadn't had an inquiry in months. He said we should reduce the price of the house. I said we would, but there wasn't anything to reduce it to.

CARRIE. Oh, somebody'll come along will like it, you'll see.

ANNA. Nobody's ever liked this house, nobody's ever going to.

CARRIE. You always get mean to the house when something worries you. What's the matter?

ANNA. And you always go to the cemetery.

CARRIE. (*Rises, enters parlor.*) No letter for two weeks. (*Crosses to L. of ANNA with bags and fan.*) I went to the main post office today, and said I was sure there'd been some confusion. Would they please call the other Berniers and see if a letter was there. And Alfie said, Carrie, there are no other Berniers in New Orleans. There are some live in Biloxi, Mississippi, with a hardware store— (*She stops suddenly, run down.*)

ANNA. Julian's busy. That's all.

(GUS, *a colored man of about thirty-five, carrying a tub of ice, enters outside.*)

GUS. (*At gate.*) You home?

ANNA. We're home. (GUS *goes off U. R. outside.*)

CARRIE. (*Puts bags in U. L. sideboard.*) I don't believe it. Never been two weeks before in his whole life. (*Softly, slowly, crossing L. of ANNA.*) I telephoned to Chicago and the hotel manager said Julian and Lily had moved months ago. Why didn't Julian tell us that?

ANNA. (*Quietly.*) I knew. I knew last week. Two letters came back here with address unknown. Carrie, Julian's married, he's moved away, he's got a business to take care of, he's busy. That's all.

CARRIE. (*Takes tea from table, crosses to window.*)

He's never been too busy to write or phone to us. You know that.

GUS. (*Enters* D. L. *outside.*) Ice box all on one side. Miss Anna, you all sure need a new ice box. You all ought to treat yourselves.

ANNA. You know, Gus, colored people are getting to talk just like white people. Kind of a shame.

GUS. (*Leaves tub* C. *and crosses to yard.*) Ought to treat yourselves. Get a new little house, new little ice box. No more Julian to worry about. Just yourselves now to treat good.

CARRIE. (*Crosses to porch.*) It's true. You getting to talk just like that white trash in my office. Just yourselves now and all that. (*With force.*) Well, what do you think? We *are* going to treat ourselves good. We're going to sell this house and never come back. We're going on a great, big, long trip. For a *year*, or five. What do you think of that?

GUS. Ought to get yourselves a cat. (*To* ANNA.) I'll water the yard for you. Where are you going this time?

CARRIE. Where we were always going. To Europe.

GUS. (*Rolling up garden hose.*) You told me that last year. And I stopped the ice. And you told me around seven years back when Julian went on his other business trip, and I stopped the ice then— (*He laughs.*) When I stop it now?

CARRIE. (*Angry, too upset.*) Very soon. *Very* soon. You hear me, Gus? *Very* soon. And if you just don't believe me you come around to church Sunday and hear us take a solemn oath right in church. We don't break a solemn oath in church.

GUS. (*Exits* U. R. *outside with hose.*) That's good. Lot of people do.

CARRIE. (*Looks at* ANNA.) Why did I tell him that about Europe?

ANNA. I don't know.

CARRIE. (*Crosses to* R. *of* ANNA.) Let's get out our travel books this evening and write out all our plans.

ANNA. No. Don't let's ever speak about it 'til we're ready to go, or think about it, or listen to each other, or tell Gus— I don't want to write things down again.

9

CARRIE. It was you who wanted to wait last time. After the wedding.

ANNA. It was you, Carrie.

CARRIE. (*Sits window seat.*) For a very good reason. Could we give them a smaller wedding present? Lily is a very rich girl and the one thing a very rich girl knows about is sterling silver. Her mother gave them ten thousand dollars. What would Lily have thought of us?

ANNA I don't know. I don't think she cares about things like that. Lily was so in love with Julian—

CARRIE. Oh, I imagine even in love you take time off to count your silver. (*Softly.*) We could still go to Europe this year. (*Rises, crosses above* ANNA.) Do you want to? How much money have we got? Did you make the deposit this week?

ANNA. $2843. No, I didn't have time.

CARRIE. (*Quickly.*) Oh, it's too hot tonight. Should we treat ourselves and go out for supper? It's been so long since we ate in a restaurant. (*Crosses and sits piano stool.*) Let's start doing our French lessons again, we'll need them now for our trip— (*She plays and sings the next speech.*)*

"Une chambre pour deux dames. Have you one room
    for two ladies?

Ah non! Trop chere! Oh, no! Too expensive!

Merci, m'sieur. Trop cheres."

We'll stay in Paris, of course, for just as long as we want. Then we'll go to Strasbourg, have the famous pate, and put flowers on the graves of Mama's relatives.

ANNA. (*Rises, crosses to porch.*) I'll have the pate. You put flowers on the graves of mama's relatives.

CARRIE. Remember the night Julian told us about the marriage? He said that night we would all go to Europe together, the way we always planned. Mama would want us to put flowers on the graves in Strasbourg. She would, Anna, and so we must.

ANNA. (*Gets newspaper, sits rocker.*) I don't know what the dead would like. Maybe Mama's changed.

CARRIE. (*Crosses to window.*) As soon as we do set a date for departure, I'll have my evening dress fixed. No

---

* *See back of book for music.*

I won't. Pink's no good for me now. I've kind of changed color as I got older. You, too. Funny to change color. (*Sings, loud and derisive.*) C'est trop chere, Monsieur— Too expensive. I don't want to go if we have to say that all the time.

ANNA. We've always said it, we always will say it. And why not?

CARRIE. I just think it would be better not to go to Europe right now.

ANNA. (*Laughs.*) We weren't going.

CARRIE. Save enough until we can go real right. That won't take long. Maybe just another year.

ANNA. A year is a long time—now.

CARRIE. If you want to go, just let's get up and go. (*In sudden, false excitement.*) Come on. Let's do. I can't tell you how much I want to go. (*Points to piano.*) That and a good piano. Every time there's a wish bone I say I want a good life for Julian, a piano, a trip to Europe. That's all. (*Crosses to* ANNA.) You know even if we can't go to Europe we could afford a little trip to Chicago. The coach fares are very cheap—

ANNA. I don't think we should run after Julian and Lily and intrude on their lives.

CARRIE. Who's doing that? What an unpleasant idea. (*As* ANNA *starts toward kitchen.*) We haven't got twenty-eight hundred and forty-three dollars. I took out a thousand dollars yesterday and sent it to Chicago. I didn't know then that Julian had moved from the hotel. But I am sure they'll forward the money—I signed the wire with love from Anna and Carrie, so he knows it comes from you, too.

ANNA. (*Slowly;* D. C.) I don't think you should have done that.

CARRIE. But I knew you would want to send it—

ANNA. How do you know what I would want?

CARRIE. (*Slowly, hurt.*) Shouldn't I know what you want for Julian? (*When* ANNA *does not answer.*) I'm sorry our trip will have to wait a little longer, but—

ANNA. I'm sorry, too. But it's not the trip. Nor the money. We are interfering, and we told ourselves we wouldn't.

11

CARRIE. But if he needs money—

ANNA. Needs it? Julian has a good business. Why do you think he needs it?

CARRIE. He's always needed it. (*Quickly.*) I mean I don't mean that. (*Sits ottoman.*) I mean it's because the letter didn't come. Anyway, even people with a good business can use a little money— You think I did wrong?

ANNA. Yes, I do.

(*She exits D. L. Outside,* GUS *enters* U. R., *gets tub and exits D. R.*)

CARRIE. (*Calling after* ANNA.) Julian won't be angry with me. (*Crosses to piano stool.*) He never has been. But perhaps I was tactless—I don't know what made me think— Why, Julian owns a whole factory. I'll just telephone to him and say— (*She makes a half move to the phone.*) But there's no place to phone to. Anna, what do you think?

(*There is no answer. After a second she moves back to the piano and begins to play. During her speech* ALBERTINE PRINE *and* HENRY SIMPSON *appear in the garden.* ALBERTINE PRINE *is a handsome woman of about forty-five, dressed with elegance, but in no current fashion. She speaks carefully, as if she were not used to talking very much. Her movements are graceful and quiet.* HENRY *is a colored man of about forty-five. He is dressed in a summer suit, but he carries a chauffeur's cap.* MRS. PRINE *stops as she hears the piano.*)

ALBERTINE. Is the older one Miss Caroline?

HENRY. (*Laughs. They are in yard* R.) They call her Carrie. No. Miss Anna is the older one.

ALBERTINE. (*Smiles.*) You laugh at me. But I only met them twice before the marriage. Two long dinners. Many savage tribes have a law that people must eat alone, in silence. Sensible, isn't it? (*She moves toward porch steps, stops.*) Perhaps it would be best if you went in. I'm not good at seeing people any more, and there

12

will be much chatter. (*He doesn't hear her. She laughs.*) Very well. But I am sure it's hot in there. Would you tell them I'm out here?

HENRY. (*Gently.*) *You* have to come to call on *them.*

ALBERTINE. Nice to live this close to the river. I still like it down here. Soggy and steaming. The flowers aren't strong enough to cover the river smells. That's the way it should be. Very vain of flowers to compete with the Mississippi. My grandmother lived on this street when I was a little girl, and I liked it then. I used to pretend I slept under the river, and had a secret morning door up into this street. What are you holding?

HENRY. A chauffeur's cap.

ALBERTINE. You win many small battles. Never mind. Wear it if you must. Put it on now and say I am here.

HENRY. No. Just go and ring the bell. (*She smiles and moves up the porch steps.* ANNA *comes back into the room, takes platter from* U. L. *and exits* D. L.)

ANNA. (*To* CARRIE.) I'm making jambalaya for you.

CARRIE. (*Turns on piano lamp.*) Isn't that nice? I like shrimp and rice better than anything. That and Bearnaise sauce. When we get to Paris I am going to have Bearnaise sauce on everything.

(*The BELL rings.* CARRIE *jumps, runs to the door.*)

ALBERTINE. (*To* CARRIE.) Hello, Miss Anna.

CARRIE. (*Amazed.*) Mrs. Prine. Mrs. Prine. Do come in. (*She moves ahead of her, calling.*) Mrs. Prine is here. Isn't that nice?

ANNA. (*Crossing to door.*) Mrs. Prine, it's gracious of you to come. We should have come to call on you.

CARRIE. (L. *of* ANNA. *Flustered.*) We're relatives now after all. We did phone, three times. But, of course, you never got the messages.

ALBERTINE. (*To* CARRIE.) Yes, I did get them, Miss Anna.

ANNA. *I* am Anna.

ALBERTINE. Forgive me.

13

ANNA. (*Turns to* CARRIE.) And this is Carrie. Close your dress.

CARRIE. (*Crosses* D. L.) Oh, my goodness. You must forgive me—

ANNA. (*Gestures toward* L. *chair.*) How are you, Mrs. Prine? Are you spending the summer across the lake?

ALBERTINE. (*Sits* L. *chair.*) No. I've closed the lake house. Now that Lily is married, I stay right here in summer. I don't like the country.

CARRIE. (*Crosses to* R. *of* ANNA.) Not like the country. My. I never heard anybody say a thing like that before. It takes courage to just up and say you don't like the country. Everybody likes the country.

ALBERTINE. Do they? I see so few people.

ANNA. (*Quickly, sitting* R. *chair.*) You must be lonely without Lily.

ALBERTINE. No.

CARRIE. Oh. Goodness.

ALBERTINE. I've come at your supper time—

ANNA. And we'd like to share it with you.

CARRIE. (*Crosses* U. C.) Oh, please do stay. I'll just go and primp myself—

ALBERTINE. No, thank you. I eat at midnight. It's my bad habit to live at night and sleep the days away.

CARRIE. Lily said that— Well, she just said that.

ALBERTINE. I suppose it was hard on a child, a young girl, not to have her mother available during the day. But perhaps it was just as well. What time do you expect Lily and Julian?

CARRIE. Expect them? Expect them? We haven't heard for seventeen days—

ALBERTINE. Lily left a message that they'd be here tonight. I came to say—

ANNA. (*As* CARRIE *turns to her.*) They'd be *here* tonight? We've had no word, Mrs. Prine.

CARRIE. (*In great excitement, moves* U. C., *then to phone, then below to* D. L.) The Chicago train comes in at seven. Have we time to get to the station? I'll phone. It's never on time. I'll get dressed right away. Are there enough shrimp and rice? Is there crayfish bisque left?

14

We can still buy some wine— Get dressed, Anna—
(ANNA *rises*.)

ALBERTINE. Miss Carrie, they are not on the Chicago
train.

CARRIE. (D. L. *of her*.) You said you had a message—

ALBERTINE. Yes, Lily spoke with Henry on the phone.
She said they would be coming here tonight.

CARRIE. Then they *must* be on that train—

ALBERTINE. No. The call was not from Chicago. The
call came from here.

CARRIE. (*Carefully*.) It could not have come from
here.

ALBERTINE. I am sure of it, Miss Carrie, because I saw
Lily two nights ago.

CARRIE. Saw her? Here? Here? (*After a second*.)
What did Lily say?

ALBERTINE. I didn't speak to her. She was moving
back and forth in front of the house as if she wished to
come in and didn't wish to come in.

CARRIE. (*After a pause*.) You saw your daughter, after
a whole year, walking in front of your house and you
didn't speak to her? I don't understand, Mrs. Prine.

ALBERTINE. That's quite all right.

ANNA. (*Softly*.) But we need to understand.

ALBERTINE. (*Turns her head, looks at* CARRIE *and
then at* ANNA.) Strange. Sometimes I can't tell which of
you is speaking. (*To* CARRIE.) Your manner, Miss Carrie, is so, well, so Southern. And then, suddenly, you are
saying what I had thought Miss Anna might say. It is as
if you had exchanged faces, back and forth, forth and
back.

CARRIE. (*Sharply*.) Did you see Julian?

ALBERTINE. There. That's what I mean. No. Julian
was not with Lily. I have simply had a message saying
they would be here this evening. I have told you all I
know.

CARRIE. (*To* ANNA.) What should we do? (*To* ALBER-
TINE.) What are you going to do?

ALBERTINE. (*Rises and crosses to porch,* ANNA *following*.) I will go home now and ask you to tell Lily
that I will come again in the morning. Please tell them

15

that the house is mostly closed up, but by tomorrow I can make them comfortable.

CARRIE. (*Crosses to porch,* L. *of* ANNA.) Oh, no. Julian will want to be here—

ALBERTINE. (R. *on porch.*) Oh, I'm sure they prefer to stay here, but . . .

ANNA. (L. *of her.*) There must be a good reason why Julian hasn't told us he is in town. If we seem upset, Mrs. Prine, it is because we are not accustomed to—

ALBERTINE. Daughters who walk in the night and mothers who do not speak to daughters who walk in the night. I really don't know why Lily didn't come in to me, nor why I didn't ask her. Good night. Thank you. (*She moves out to gate.* HENRY *is waiting in the garden.* ALBERTINE *moves toward him, turns toward the porch.*) I think you have met Henry Simpson. Miss Anna and Miss Carrie Berniers, Henry.

HENRY. Good evening. (ALBERTINE *takes his arm and they exit.*)

CARRIE. (*Softly.*) Is *that* the man Lily calls Henry? *That* man was there in a white coat when we went for dinner, but I didn't know that was the Henry. You mean he's a Nigra? (*Crosses* D. R. *in garden.*) I never heard anybody introduce a nigra before. I'm sorry I didn't say something. I never think of things in time. (*She turns, sees* ANNA *has gone back to the living room, moves to join her.*) That man Lily called Henry is a nigra. Is he a chauffeur? What is he? Last time, he was a butler. Introduces us to a nigra— Do you believe that strange woman? Do you believe they're in town?

ANNA. (*At* C.) Maybe Lily's pregnant. They arrived and wanted to go to a doctor first so they could tell us the good news. I'm sure something like that—

CARRIE. (*At window.*) She's not pregnant.

ANNA. How do you know?

CARRIE. Girls like Lily don't have babies right away. Too full of good times the first year of marriage, I can tell you that.

ANNA. What do you know about the first year of marriage?

CARRIE. I just know.

16

ANNA. (*Crosses to* D. L.) How? From books you don't read any more?

CARRIE. You're saying that again. Teasing me again. No, I don't read much any more, and I don't play the piano, or put ice on my face, or walk for wild flowers— (*Very loudly, as if she were going to cry.* ANNA *sets up bridge table* D. L. C.) I get tired now after work and that terrible man. (*Gets silverware* U. R. *sideboard.*) All I want to do is have a little something to eat and play casino, and— Don't you like to play casino with me, is that what you're saying?

ANNA. (*Takes silverware from her.*) Not every night. I like to read—

CARRIE. You don't ever have to play casino again. Read whenever you like, but don't nag me about it. You used to do it with Julian, too. Some people read and some people learn other ways— I think she's crazy, that Mrs. Prine. And you know what? I don't believe they're in New Orleans without coming here. (*Lamely.*) Do you? What do you think?

ANNA. I think it's happened again. And he feels bad and doesn't want to tell us.

CARRIE. Well, that's natural enough. Who wants to come home and say they've failed? What do you mean? *What's* happened again?

ANNA. (*Gently.*) You understand me. (*Exits toward kitchen.*)

CARRIE. (*But* ANNA *has left the room.*) A great many men take a long time to find themselves. And a lot of *good* businessmen just aren't worth bowing to. (ANNA *comes back carrying a tray of food.*) Are you going to eat?

ANNA. I always have. I think it's best to continue.

CARRIE. (*Sits ottoman.*) You're just as worried and nervous as I am. You always talk cold when you get nervous. Anna. Please. When he comes, don't be cold. Please. It will hurt him—

ANNA. Why do you so often make it seem as if I had always been severe and unloving? I don't think it's true. (*Leans tray against* C. *table.*)

17

CARRIE. I don't believe I do that. It's you who gave him everything, long before I was old enough to help.

ANNA. (*Takes a bank book from her pocket.*) Here is the savings bank book. Give it to him.

CARRIE. (*Deeply pleased. Rises.*) Oh, thank you. I'll give it to him when we're alone and Lily doesn't see. (ANNA *sits at the table.* CARRIE *moves about.*) It's only for a short time. We'll have it back. After all, in a sense, this money is his. We lent it to him and he paid us back. This is the very money he paid us back, Anna. So, in a sense, it's his.

ANNA. Do come and eat. (*Places piano stool L. of table.*)

CARRIE. (*At window.*) You're thinking that what I just said is foolish. You're thinking that you never understood where he got the money to pay for your operation—

ANNA. You know very well where he got it: He played in a dangerous poker game.

CARRIE. I'm not so sure. I often wondered—

ANNA. The shrimp's getting cold. (*She begins to eat.*)

CARRIE. I can't eat. I don't know how you can. (*Sighs, then brightens.*) You know, it sounds strange, but I am positive he will make a fortune someday.

ANNA. A fortune isn't necessary. A job is. (*Serves herself.*)

CARRIE. All those self-made men at the office. Like Mr. Barrett. No interest in anything. Making fun of opera and poetry and women. Mean, too, ever since he tried to put his hands on me years ago. Pig. Things can go wrong for a long time and then suddenly everything in a man's life clears up— Have you a headache, Anna? Do your eyes worry you tonight? Can I get you something?

ANNA. I haven't a headache. And if I had I wouldn't know the remedy. A prescription put up fresh each time Julian fails.

CARRIE. (U. L. *of her.*) Oh, don't be sad. I'm not. I feel cheerful. Place and people and time make things go wrong, and then all of a sudden— (*There is the Offstage noise of a CAR DOOR SLAM. She jumps up, runs to*

18

the door, stares out, nods at what she sees. Slowly, suddenly cool and calm, she turns back to ANNA.) I am going to wait on the porch. Please don't show what you feel. Welcome him as he should always be welcomed in this, his house. (*She moves out to the porch.*)

(JULIAN'S *voice is heard Offstage.*)

JULIAN. Is that my Carrie on the porch?
CARRIE. (*Laughs with enormous pleasure.*) Yes, that's your Carrie on the porch. I can still jump. Shall I jump and you will catch me? (*In the middle of her speech, in a preparatory-jump movement, a* TAXI DRIVER *appears carrying a very large number of packages covered by a raincoat. He puts them on porch, exits out gate.*) Oh.

(JULIAN BERNIERS *and* LILY BERNIERS *appear. He is a handsome, tall man of about thirty-four.* LILY *is a frail, pretty girl of about twenty-one. She moves behind him.* JULIAN'S *arms and hands are filled with a banjo case and packages.*)

JULIAN. Don't jump. I have no hands to catch you. (*Grinning, he puts packages and case* R. *of garden bench and moves up the steps as* CARRIE *waits for him. He takes her in his arms, lifting her from the ground.*) Darling Carrie-Pie.
CARRIE. Julian. (*He kisses her, puts her down. She clings to him a minute and follows him as he moves quickly into the house and toward* ANNA.)
JULIAN. Anna! (LILY *holds* D. L. *in yard, puts down wicker basket.* ANNA *stands waiting for* JULIAN, *smiling warmly. When he kisses* ANNA *it is quite different—no less warm, but different—from his greeting to* CARRIE. ANNA *moves away from him and to* LILY, *who comes to meet her at door.*)
ANNA. My dear Lily, how good to see you. (*Kisses her.*)
CARRIE. (*To* JULIAN.) One year and six days. (*As she hears* ANNA'S *greeting to* LILY *at door.*) Lily! I didn't
19

see you. Forgive me. One year and six days. I was so
excited that I didn't see you—

JULIAN. (*To* TAXI DRIVER, *who comes in carrying two
valises.*) Bring them in. Bring them in. (*Holds door
open.*) I'm hungry, Anna. Hungry for your cooking. Not
a good restaurant in Chicago. Would *not* know a red
pepper if they saw one.

CARRIE. (U. C.) There's crayfish in the icebox, thank
God, and shrimp and rice on the table—

JULIAN. (R. *of her.*) Then go and get them. I'm weak.
Very, very weak.

ANNA. (*Laughs from porch.*) You don't look it.

CARRIE. Sit down, dear—

(*She starts to run off to kitchen. Before she does,* JULIAN
hands the TAXI DRIVER *several bills. She peers at
them.* JULIAN *laughs.*)

JULIAN. Don't be nosey.

TAXI DRIVER. (*Stares at the bills.*) Thank you, sir.

JULIAN. He deserves them. (*Another bill.*)

TAXI DRIVER. Thank you—

JULIAN. No porters at the station because the train
came in early.

TAXI DRIVER. (*Puzzled.*) The train came in—

JULIAN. (*Quickly.*) All right. Good-bye. (*Gives him
another bill and moves him out door to* C. *below steps.*)
Buy your baby something from me. And name the next
one Julian.

(TAXI DRIVER *laughs and exits.*)

ANNA. (D. R. *on porch.* LILY *has entered parlor to*
U. C.) You still say that to waiters and taxi drivers?
That means you've been in a poker game. And what train
came in early?

CARRIE. (*Very quickly, opens door for* ANNA *and*
JULIAN *to enter.*) Anna, go get the crayfish. And make
fresh, hot coffee. Lily, shall I take you to your room?
Oh, my no, it needs cleaning. Well, just sit down.
(*Crosses* L.) Anna, get the crayfish for Julian.

20

ANNA. (*Turns on chandelier.*) There are no crayfish.

JULIAN. (R. *of her.*) We'll go out later and have them with champagne. (*To* ANNA.) The same dress?

ANNA. The same dress. You look tired, Lily. Can I get you something?

LILY. (L. *of her.*) I am tired. Julian doesn't like me to be tired.

JULIAN. (*Circles below to* L. *of table, picks up* ANNA's *plate.*) I don't like anybody to be tired. But it was a long trip, darling— (*As if he is prompting her.*) Wasn't it a long trip, Lily?

LILY. Yes. When it happened. It was long when it happened.

JULIAN. Lily.

LILY. (*Quickly to* CARRIE *and* ANNA.) It was a very long trip. Longer than going. (JULIAN *sits* L. *chair, starts to eat.*)

ANNA. The wedding day. My, how it rained.

LILY. (*Smiling, suddenly uplifted, happy.*) Did it rain? I don't remember. It was all days to me: Cold and hot days, fog and light, and I was on a high hill running down with the top of me, and flying with the left of me, and singing with the right of me— (*Softly, as if she is worn out.*) I was doing everything nice anybody had ever done nice.

ANNA. (*Touched.*) Nice.

LILY. (*Crosses to window seat.*) What were you doing when I was doing all that, Julian?

JULIAN. (*His mouth very full.*) Being my kind of happy.

LILY. You're always happy.

JULIAN. I am glad you think that, darling.

ANNA. (*Above* R. *chair.*) You've given us no news. How is the shoe factory?

JULIAN. What shoe factory?

(LILY *sits window seat, puts her things down. There is a long silence.* JULIAN *is grinning and eating.* CARRIE, *standing behind* JULIAN, *holds up her hand in an attempt to stop* ANNA's *questions.* ANNA *sees it and ignores it.*)

21

ANNA. (*Carefully.*) The shoe factory that you bought in Chicago.

JULIAN. Oh, *that* shoe factory. It's gone.

ANNA. Don't be flip with me, Julian.

CARRIE. (*Gesturing wildly.*) He's not. He's just trying to explain—

JULIAN. (*Turns, sees* CARRIE, *laughs, catches the gesturing hand. Rises.*) No, I'm not. I'm not trying to explain anything. (*To* ANNA.) I was being flip. I forget that you worry about the money I lose.

ANNA. It's not the money— It's that you don't seem to care. And the money was—

JULIAN. Lily's money. (*Crosses* U. L.)

LILY. My money? Doesn't matter about my money. I don't want money.

CARRIE. (*Crossing to* LILY.) You mustn't worry about it. Not worth it.

LILY. I'm not worried about money, Miss Carrie.

CARRIE. I suppose rich people always worry about money. People like us have to learn there are more important things.

LILY. I said I wasn't worried about money, Miss Carrie.

CARRIE. Well, you mustn't.

JULIAN. (*To* ANNA. *Puts plate on table* D. L.) The factory was a crooked sell. The machinery wasn't any good. I didn't know anything about shoe machinery and I never should have thought I did. Man who sold it to me faked the books. That's all.

CARRIE. (*Softly.*) That could happen to anybody.

JULIAN. (*Laughs.*) No. Not to anybody. Just to me.

CARRIE. (*Crosses to him.*) That's not true. And you mustn't ever believe it.

JULIAN. Darling Carrie. Hiding her hopes that I would come home with Chicago over my shoulder, dressed in pure gold, bringing candied oranges to hang in your hair. Well, that's just what I've done. Your hair don't look nice, Carrie-Pie.

ANNA. (*Crosses to pile dishes on tray.*) We can help you.

22

CARRIE. (*Crosses to* L. *of* JULIAN.) Yes, indeed we can. Julian, come in the kitchen and help me wash the dishes.

JULIAN. No, Ma'am. And you're never going to wash dishes again.

ANNA. (*Holds tray of dishes.*) I don't wish to ask questions that you might not like, Julian. But it's uncomfortable this way. Your mother was here, Lily. She said she had seen you, had a message from you. She said she would come back tomorrow. (*To* JULIAN *who has turned to stare at* LILY.) So this is not your first night in town. You need not explain, but I thought we should. (LILY *crosses to yard.*)

JULIAN. We've been in New Orleans for a week, at the hotel. I had a good reason for that. It was no neglect of you. I even came by and stared in at you—the first hour back. You were playing casino and Anna was yawning. You look tired, both of you. You need a long, long good time. (*To* ANNA.) This time, no need to be sad. (*He crosses to door.*) I used to tell you: never was any good; never came out anywhere.

ANNA. I am sad that you think it all so easy, so unimportant, so— "Never came out anywhere." I guess not, although I don't think those words mean very much. (JULIAN *moves out to porch.*)

CARRIE. (*To* ANNA, *in a voice used once before.*) I won't have that kind of talk. This is a happy, joyous night. Julian is home and that's all we need to know. It's a happy, joyous night. (ANNA *exits* D. L., *taking table.*)

LILY. (*To* JULIAN.) I didn't see my mother, I didn't go in. And I only sent the message today. I knew we'd arrive here, anyway, so— (*Softly, when there is no answer.*) I disobeyed you. But not much. Have I done harm?

JULIAN. (L. *of her.*) No.

(CARRIE, *listening, pretending she isn't, is idly playing on the piano with one hand.*)

LILY. I know you told me not to see anybody. But you didn't tell me why or anything. You just kept leaving the hotel. I want to see my mother. I want to talk with my mother.

JULIAN. (*Smiles.*) I'm glad to hear that. I've never heard you want that before.

LILY. Are you angry with me?

JULIAN. No. (*Smiles at her, shakes his head, moves away.*) Carrie, stop that awful sound, darling. Just wait for the good piano—

CARRIE. (*Laughs.*) No, I'd only find out I couldn't really play.

JULIAN. (*Has moved out to porch and is hauling in valises. LILY rises and follows him. He enters, picks up his valise, moves U. C.*) You all been to the opera?

CARRIE. (*Crosses to R. of him.*) No. We'll wait until Europe.

JULIAN. (*Laughs.*) Still talking about Europe?

CARRIE. (*Taking valise from him.*) Oh, we'll go some day. You'll see.

JULIAN. Some day soon?

CARRIE. In a few years. Plenty of time. We're not that old. (*She moves quickly out of the room U. C. to R.*)

JULIAN. Yes, you are. Old enough to have fun. Have to crowd it in now, Carrie, both of you. Crowd it in fast. (*Smiling at LILY as he crosses to porch, then to boxes D. R.*) You, too. Twenty-one is very, very old.

LILY. (*Crosses to him on porch.*) Tell me you're not angry with me.

JULIAN. (*His arms heavy with boxes, gives one box to LILY.*) I am not angry with you. Have I ever been angry with you? Why do you ask me that so often?

LILY. (*As she steps aside.*) Julian, who is the lady you talked to on the train?

JULIAN. (*Too lightly.*) Which lady— I talk to everybody.

LILY. The not such a young lady with the sad face.

JULIAN. (*Picks up two boxes and banjo.*) Most ladies on trains are not so young and have sad faces. I often wondered why. (*He tries to pass her.*) Move, darling.

LILY. The one you were with yesterday and Sunday and—

JULIAN. (*Turns, stares at her.*) Where did you see me?

24

LILY. I don't know. Just on the street. In front of the hotel—

JULIAN. No, you didn't.

LILY. No, I didn't. That's the first lie I ever told you, Julian.

JULIAN. Then it's one more than I ever told ycu. (*Carrying boxes, he moves into living room.* LILY *follows him.*)

LILY. I saw you in Audubon Park. On a bench. By the ducks.

JULIAN. (*Puts banjo on piano, boxes Upstage of it.*) Have you told anybody?

LILY. No.

JULIAN. Don't. The lady would be in trouble. And so would we.

LILY. And in that little restaurant. At a table—

JULIAN. Oh, Lily.

LILY. (*Crosses, gets hat and coat on window seat, picks up her valise.*) I didn't mean to walk after you, to follow you. But I was so lonely in the hotel room, locked up the way you asked me to be.

JULIAN. All right, darling, all right. Don't follow me, Lily, ever again. That's not the way to be married. (LILY *hesitates, as if to say something, then exits.* JULIAN *begins to arrange room for gift giving. Puts box on* L. *chair, above piano.*) Hey, everybody. Come and get your presents. Hey, where is everybody?

CARRIE. (*Appears in the garden, runs up the porch, speaks in a whisper.*) Julian. I want to speak to you. Come here.

JULIAN. Can't. You come here.

CARRIE. Ssssssh. (*She sits down on the porch steps.*) Come here. I've got a nice secret. And this is where we always told nice secrets.

JULIAN. You come here. *I* got nice secrets. Where's Anna? Anna!

CARRIE. Ssh. Ssh.

JULIAN. (*Crosses to porch and sits beside her.*) What's the matter with you?

CARRIE. (*Gives him the bank-book.*) No need for Lily to see. You'll just tell her it's yours. More than twenty-eight hundred dollars. And we don't need any of it, not any of it, so don't say anything— (*He takes her hands, kisses them. She is very moved. Softly, embarrassed.*) Don't say anything, please. And if that isn't enough, we can manage other things, too.

JULIAN. (*Stares at the book, then rises and calls out.*) Anna!

CARRIE. Anna doesn't want any thanks— (ANNA *comes into the room to* D. L.)

JULIAN. (*Enters the room, holds out the book.*) God bless you. All my life it's been this way.

ANNA. (*Smiles.*) You are our life. It is we who should thank you.

JULIAN. (*He takes her in his arms.*) How many, many times?

CARRIE. (*Comes into room, to* R. *of him.*) You paid it back, always.

JULIAN. You know I didn't. But this time I will.

CARRIE. Of course you will. But Lily doesn't have to know about all this— So ssh.

JULIAN. Stop ssshing me and come here and sit down and stop talking. (*He seats* CARRIE *on piano stool* D. L., *motions* ANNA *to be seated* L. *chair. Takes raincoat off boxes. Gives box of gloves to each, then brings a double-depth box to floor* D. C. *He pulls from it two fancy evening dresses. They are too grand for anything less than a ball.* CARRIE *leans forward, stares at them.*) For a ball. (*Gives dress to* ANNA.) Wear them the second time at the opera, if you like. (*Gives dress to* CARRIE.) But I don't think dresses like these should be worn twice in the same city, do you? Everybody in Paris will talk, and we can't have that. (*He opens another box on* C. *table.*) Maybe you can wear them again when you get to Strasbourg. (*Points his finger at* CARRIE.) Not to the cemetery. I bet the opera house there is draughty— (*He has taken out a fur piece; gives it to* ANNA.) No, no. I've got things mixed up. (*He begins to fumble in another box.*) Or so the lady said. The furs are for breakfast or something. (*He is now holding up two velvet, fur-trimmed opera coats from double-depth box. Places fur box* D. C. *They are royal in feeling.*) These are for the dresses. And

26

maybe they can be worn the second time. (*He moves to arrange them over* ANNA *and* CARRIE. CARRIE'S *is much too large and she looks drowned. He gets two boxes from above piano, gives one to each.*) Suits for travelling. Dresses for informal evenings, whatever that is. (*Pulls out frothy, very young negligee.*) For flirtations on Italian terraces. (*Drapes it over* CARRIE. *Gives* CARRIE *a jewel box.*) Garnets. Your birthstone. Next time, pearls. (*Gets a hat out of a hatbox and puts it on* ANNA'S *head. Gives* ANNA *a large gold mesh bag.*) Remember when old lady Senlis used to come along swinging her gold mesh bag, and your eyes would pop out wondering what was in it? Look and see what's in this one.

ANNA. (*Softly.*) What is all this, Julian?

JULIAN. (R. *of her.*) It is that we're rich. Just open your gold mesh bag with diamond initials—Anna, *diamond* initials—and see what's inside.

CARRIE. (*Loud, nervous giggle; rises.*) The only thing could be, is a certificate to an insane asylum.

JULIAN. (*Takes an envelope from the purse.*) You're wrong. A certificate to a boat called the Ottavia, sailing day after tomorrow. Two rooms, one of them a parlor. Think of that, a parlor on a boat. (*He takes the envelope to* CARRIE.) Look at it, look at it. Of course, we had always planned to go together. But I won't be able to go with you, darling, not this time, big business here, and all that. (CARRIE *sits piano stool.*) But we'll join you in a few months—

CARRIE. (*Dully.*) We'll wait for you.

JULIAN. No, you won't. No more waiting for anything.

ANNA. (*Softly places gift clothes* D. C. *on boxes. Leaves cape on chair* L.) Where does all this come from, Julian?

JULIAN. All over town . . . I just went in places and said bring out the best for two pretty ladies who are on their way. On their way.

ANNA. (*Crosses* U. R. C.) You know what I mean.

JULIAN. (*Brings her cape, puts it over her shoulders.*) I know what you mean. They were bought with my money. Mine. Yours. Ours. We're rich. How do you like that, how do you like it?

CARRIE. (*Crosses to box on* C. *table.*) We'll like it fine—when it happens. (*Giggles.*) Rich. Us!

JULIAN. What are you doing? (*Moves* L. C.)

CARRIE. Trying to make a neat package. (*Packing negligee.*)

JULIAN. Stop it. (*When she doesn't, he pulls box away.*) I said to stop it. Nothing's going back this time. Listen to me. Now listen to me. We're rich. (LILY *comes into the room. She is in her slip and is carrying a hairbrush. He smiles at her.*) Aren't we rich? (*Crosses to her.*)

LILY. Mama's rich, I guess.

JULIAN. No, us, us. I've been telling you for a week.

LILY. There are three men at the back door. From a trucking company—

JULIAN. Tell them to bring them in, darling. (*She exits.*) Right in here. Now you're going to see something.

CARRIE. (*Stares at the boat tickets.*) Are these real boat tickets? I mean, stamped and bought?

JULIAN. Bought and stamped. Look. It's going to be this way. The first money is for us to have things. Have fun. After that, I promise you, we'll invest. And like all people with money we'll make more and more and more until we get sick from it. Rich people get sick more than we do. Maybe from worry. (*Moves* L. *chair to above piano.*)

ANNA. Poor people, too. Like me, right now. (*Very sharply.*) Where did you get this money, Julian?

CARRIE. Oh, now don't start that tone. You know very well he's been in a poker game.

JULIAN. (U. C.) No, she doesn't know that, and you don't either. (*A truckman rolls in a large refrigerator.*) Come in. Just put it there. (*Motions to* ANNA.) By that lady. (*Two* MEN *carry in a fancy, highly carved spinet. There is a big sign on the spinet lettered "CARRIE."*) And put that by this lady.

CARRIE. My God!

JULIAN. (*He crosses* D. R. *and pulls out several large bills. Motions* FIRST MAN *down to him.*) Thank you.

Buy the babies something from me. Name the next one Julian.

FIRST MAN. There ain't going to be no next one. Thank you.

(*The* THREE MEN *exit* U. C. *to* R. ANNA *crosses* D. L.)

LILY. (*At* C.) Why do you always say that? We'll name our son Julian. Don't you believe—

JULIAN. (*Laughs.*) Insurance. That's all.

CARRIE. (*To* LILY, *who retreats to door.*) You're in your slip. In front of men.

JULIAN. Can't harm them. (*Crosses to spinet, places bench in front of it.*)

CARRIE. I never heard of such a thing. Answering the door in your underwear. Don't you mind?

JULIAN. (*Takes her to spinet.*) I mind that you haven't looked at your piano. Think, Carrie, a fine new piano, what you always wanted, right in front of you— Play it. Play it for me, Carrie, the way we used to always say. (*She puts out her hand, touches a note, takes her hand away and puts it over her face.* JULIAN *is* R. *of her; softly, smiling.*) I know. Take your time. (*He looks around, sees* ANNA, *laughs.*)

ANNA. What is all this? Answer me, please, Julian.

JULIAN. (U. C.) I'm going to tell you all about it some day soon. I can't now. But I'll tell you this much, I didn't play poker. All I did was sell some real estate.

ANNA. (D. L.) You never owned any real estate.

JULIAN. No. But I do now, see?

ANNA. No, I don't see. I don't see at all.

JULIAN. Once I liked somebody and they liked me, and she thought I was kind to her. So years go by and she hears about a good thing, and gives me the tip on it. And the tip works. (*Crosses* D. R.) Boy, how it worked. Now let it go. I'll tell you soon, but in the meantime I gave my word because she could be in bad trouble. Now stop worrying, and sit back—I finished the deal and collected the money at two o'clock today. At two-eighteen, I rang the bell of Mr. Maxwell Shine. (ANNA *sits piano stool.*) And so here's the mortgage to the

29

house. (*Softly, kneels* R. *of her.*) Look, Anna, first time in our lives, first time in our father's life. You have a house, without worry or asking him to wait. Remember when I was a kid and the time you took me with you and you made me tell Mr. Shine how I wouldn't have any place to live unless— Christ God, how I hated— Do you remember?

ANNA. I remember.

JULIAN. Well, there'll never be such things to say again. Not for any of us. (*He shouts; rises to* C.) Not ever, ever. (*Crosses; to Carrie, who has crossed to refrigerator.*) I wrote your Mr. Barrett a letter last night. I wrote it three times. "Your petty angers, the silk stockings at Christmas that were always cheaper than a decent salary— Miss Caroline Berniers will not return to work." (CARRIE *makes a sound in her throat, stands staring at him. He turns to* ANNA.) For you I just wrote that Miss Anna Berniers was resigning from the coat department because she was leaving for an extended European tour. (ANNA *lifts her head and stares at him. There is a long silence.*) Well. Say something.

ANNA. I can't say something.

JULIAN. I know, I know. All came so fast. Well, we don't have to say things to each other, never did. Just sit back and have fun. That's all I want. (*To* LILY.) And for you— Give me the wedding ring. (*Crosses to her by phone* R. *Sharply she pulls back from him.*) Give it to me. (*He takes the ring from her finger.*) Twenty dollars in a pawnshop, and I polished it, and prayed you wouldn't mind, or say anything. (*He takes from his pocket and puts on her finger, a very large diamond ring.*) With this, I you wed again, and forever.

LILY. Please give me my ring.

JULIAN. (*Holds up her hand to show her the new diamond.*) Look, darling, look at it. Superstitious? (LILY *starts to cry, steps Upstage. He looks at* LILY, *then at* CARRIE, *then at* ANNA.) Please don't cry, or look it, all of you. (*He takes an envelope from his pocket, goes to each of them as he speaks, lets them look into the envelope.*) One hundred and fifty thousand dollars, less peanuts— (*Motions to the packages.* LILY *sits window seat.*) for this. Seventy-five thousand for my partner, seventy-five thousand for me. My lawyer said I shouldn't carry all that cash around, rich people don't carry cash not more than ten or twenty dollars, so other people pay the bills. But I said I'll carry this, I like it— Hey, did you hear—my lawyer. *I've* got a *lawyer*. What do you think of that? (CARRIE *has paid little attention to the money in the envelope, but* ANNA *is staring at it.*) Ain't counterfeit. (*Crosses to* CARRIE.) Twenty, five thousand dollar bills, fifty, one thousand dollar bills— (*Crosses to* ANNA.) You'll believe it all by tomorrow. Big, successful Julian, the way you wanted me. (*Sits on spinet.*) The man who was never good at anything except living on his sisters, and losing his wife's money. I never minded failure much, you minded. (CARRIE *crosses to porch, sits rocker.*) But you know what? I like things this way: Making bargains, talking big— I don't take my hat off in elevators any more. (*Laughs with great pleasure. He crosses to yard and picks up a large basket.*) Now to *important* business. Last night I drew up a budget list, you know, the way we used to. Only where we put carfare for the week, I put champagne, and where we put lunch money, sixty cents each, I put caviar. (*Crosses to her.*) You'll like caviar.

CARRIE. I hate caviar.

JULIAN. (*Holds up the basket.*) Champagne.

CARRIE. The one time I ever ate it, I hated it.

JULIAN. *And* caviar, Carrie-Pie.

CARRIE. Just hated it.

JULIAN. You'll learn to like it. (*He starts toward kitchen.*) We're going to have a champagne-caviar party just for us. Sit down and play the piano. (*He exits* D. L.)

CARRIE. (*Crosses after him to* C. *in parlor. Softly.*) Since when do you give me orders? (*Very loudly.*) I said since when do you give me orders? (ANNA *puts up a hand, as if to quiet her.*) I don't believe it all. I don't believe it. (*When* ANNA *doesn't answer her.*) We have no jobs. (*To* LILY.) What is this all about?

LILY. I want my ring. I was married in my ring.

CARRIE. I asked you a question, Lily.

LILY. I didn't hear you.

CARRIE. What is this all about? Where did Julian get this money?

LILY. I don't know, ma'm. A lady came to Chicago and phoned him, and he went to see her, and everything changed and he said we were coming here, and she was on the train, and he didn't want me to know. She calls him every night at six o'clock.

CARRIE. I'm not talking about women. That's not my business. I'm talking about this— (*She motions around.*) Europe day after tomorrow! Has he gone crazy? What does he think we are, fine ladies with maids and secretaries who can move whenever they like? Streetwalkers' clothes. I wouldn't be seen in this. (*Throws clothes and hat on pile* D. C.) Not seen in them. (*Turns on* ANNA.) For God's sake take off that stuff. What are you doing?

ANNA. (*Who is reading the mortgage document.*) Trying to understand.

CARRIE. (*In a whisper.*) Does it really say—

ANNA. Yes. It really says we own this house.

CARRIE. This house. This awful house. He's changed. He even talks different. Didn't he know we hated this house, always, always, always.

ANNA. You used to tell him how much we liked it, and the garden, and the street, and the memories of Mama and Papa.

CARRIE. You know very well I said all that to keep him from being ashamed of the house and what we didn't have—

ANNA. (*Hands her the paper and crosses to door.*) Well. We've been rewarded.

LILY. I want my ring. I was married in my ring. (*She holds up her hand.*) This is a vulgar ring.

CARRIE. (*Points to a tiny pin she is wearing.*) Topaz is my birthstone. How could he forget when he gave me this pin with the first job he ever lost. I even wear it at night—

LILY. I want my married ring.

CARRIE. (*Crosses to spinet.*) You said that before.

(*Phone rings.* ANNA *moves toward it, but* LILY *answers.*)

32

LILY. Hello. (*A slight pause.*) No, ma'm. No, he isn't. This is his wife. What is *your* name?

(*She stares at the phone and then hangs up. After a second, she throws the diamond to the floor. JULIAN enters with a tray containing bottle of champagne, four glasses partly filled, caviar and crackers.*)

JULIAN. (*Puts tray on refrigerator.*) I heard the phone. Didn't the phone ring?

ANNA. (*After a second.*) No. (*Sits ottoman.*)

JULIAN. Now. (*To* CARRIE, *points to piano.*) Why aren't you playing? And you took off— Put the pretty clothes on so I can be proud.

CARRIE. (*Sharply.*) All of them?

LILY. The phone did ring. It was that lady who calls every evening. I told her you weren't here. I don't know why I said it, but I did.

JULIAN. (*Crosses to her.*) I have business with that lady. I've told you that before. I was to meet her this evening. It's not easy for her to call me and I can't call her. Did she say she'd call back tonight? (LILY *shakes her head.*) Why did you tell her I wasn't here?

LILY. I didn't know I was going to do it. Please forgive me. It wasn't nice.

JULIAN. Not nice, wasn't it? You know what I think it wasn't? Respectful. (*He moves toward* CARRIE. LILY *sits window seat.*) Re—spect—ful— Respectful. I don't think I can spell that word. I never used it before. But I like it. (*He hits his chest.*) A man. Respect. That's what you always said, success isn't everything but it makes a man stand straight, and you were right. (*He hands a glass of champagne to* ANNA. *He speaks to* CARRIE.) You want to know something? I bring you a piano, I ask you to play it for me, you don't. I don't think that's respectful. (*He laughs.*) I like that word. (CARRIE *sits down at the piano and begins to play. She fumbles, as if she is thinking of something else, then plays a waltz.* JULIAN *moves to* LILY, *gives her a glass.*) I forgive you, my infant bride. (*He looks at her hand.*) Where's your ring? (ANNA *rises, crosses, picks up the ring.*)

33

LILY. I don't know.

JULIAN. You don't know?

ANNA. I have it. I was looking at it. (JULIAN *gets ring, puts it on* LILY's *finger. Kisses her.*)

(*The music stops sharply and he turns to* CARRIE.)

JULIAN. More, more. It's a party. (CARRIE *plays again.*) We're having a party. (*To* ANNA.) Dance? (*He pulls her to her feet, whirls her around, the long evening coat tangled in her legs.*)

CARRIE. (*Stops playing, rises.*) Anna. You look like a fool. Like a real fool. (ANNA *pulls away from* JULIAN *to* D. L.)

JULIAN. (C.) What's the matter? (*Sings.*) "Une chambre, pour deux dames. Have you one room for two ladies?" Non, ils ne sont pas trop chere. Nothing is too expensive now. Send up two pounds de caviar pour breakfast pour ma sister et moi. (*He leans over her with a spoonful of caviar.*) Now. (*He forces her mouth open. She pulls away, smearing her face with caviar. He laughs.*)

CARRIE. You're laughing at me. You've never laughed at me before. (*She rises, shrilly.*) You're laughing at me.

JULIAN. No, I wasn't. I'm just happy. I'm giving a party— (*He looks at* ANNA *who has her head hung; at* LILY *who looks sad and tearful.*) What's the matter with everybody? (*Crosses to* D. R. C.) We're not having a very nice party. What's the matter?

CURTAIN

ACT TWO

The next morning. ANNA *enters* U. L. *with a pair of shoes, which she puts on piano stool,* D. L. *Already on stool are polish and a rag. She takes camellia plant out to garden urn. Returns to window and reaches through for second plant.*

CARRIE. (*Enters* D. L. *with coffee pot and cup and saucer.*) Is your headache better?

ANNA. (*On porch.*) I didn't have a headache.

CARRIE. (*Fills cup. Leaves pot on* C. *table.*) You said you did.

ANNA. (*Puts plant* L. *of porch steps in yard.*) No, I didn't.

CARRIE. (*Crosses to porch.*) Last night, before you went to bed, you said your eyes were bothering you, you had a headache.

ANNA. No. (*Enters parlor, removes things from stool and sits on it.*)

CARRIE. I think everybody's going crazy. I really do. (*Enters parlor to* U. C.) No wonder you can't remember what you said. I don't think I slept an hour. I'd close my eyes, and say I don't believe it, when I get up (*Points to spinet, to boxes, etc.*) that thing, and that, won't be there, and it will be years ago. He stayed out in the garden drinking by himself 'til late last night. (*Points* U. R. C.) Still asleep?

ANNA. I suppose so.

CARRIE. How could *you* have slept last night? Mama used to say you could sleep through anything.

ANNA. (*Polishing shoes.*) Mama believed that lack of sleep was a sign of good breeding. Do you remember the time she said she hadn't slept for two years? (*Points inside.*) Yes, I heard Lily, if that's what you mean.

CARRIE. She rattled around half the night. She went out, she came back, she went out. She's a very strange

35

girl. I remember thinking that the first time I ever met her. (*Gets handbag* U. L. *and points around the room.*) And she doesn't know any more about all this than we do. That's not natural in a good marriage. In a good marriage a man doesn't have secrets from his wife. (*Crosses to window.*)

ANNA. How do you know?

CARRIE. (*Puts on lipstick.*) It's not natural in a good marriage, I can tell you that. (*Leaves bag on window seat.*)

ANNA. We don't know anything about a good marriage or a bad one. I read somewhere that old maids are the true detectives of the human heart. But I don't want to be a detective of other people's hearts. I'm having enough trouble with my own.

CARRIE. (*Crosses for coffee.*) I know you are. I know you're just as worried as I am. I know that's why you're having headaches again.

ANNA. I said I didn't have a headache.

CARRIE. (*Crosses* U. R.) I'll get you something for it. (*After a pause.*) Julian pampers Lily as if she were a child. (*Crosses* D. C.) He never treated us that way, always boasted of our good sense.

ANNA. He didn't marry us.

CARRIE. Nobody wants a child for a wife.

ANNA. There's no sense telling your opinions about marriage to me. I don't know anything about it. (*She picks up valise.*)

CARRIE. What are you doing?

ANNA. Put your clothes out. I'm going to wash and iron today.

CARRIE. What for? (*Gets bag from window, crosses to door.*)

ANNA. (*Turns to stare at her.*) Europe. (*Puts valise on* L. *chair. Opens it.*)

CARRIE. We'll miss the eight-thirty street car. (*When there is no answer.*) we'll miss the eight-thirty street car. (*When there is no answer, crosses above to* L. *of her.*) I know what Julian said. But I get the mail before Mr. Barrett, and if Julian did write such a letter I'll just throw it out. You better go down to the store and get somebody to do the same for you. (*Very sharply, when* ANNA *does not answer, slams shut top of valise.*) *We have no jobs.* They're not easy to get and we're not young. You told me all my life what that would mean to us. You said that as long as we could work and save a little then we could get sick when we were old, and take care of Julian, and not end as Mama and Papa did.

ANNA. (*Packs clothes from* L. *chair.*) Julian has come home rich. We can get sick now.

CARRIE. Rich! Do you really believe this foolishness? Julian rich! God knows what he's been up to. God knows when and how it will blow up. Doesn't it worry you?

ANNA. Yes. It worries me. But I think we should go to Europe. He wants us to go.

CARRIE. (*Crosses to window.*) What do you mean, he wants us to go? You make it sound as if we're in his way.

ANNA. (*Crosses* U. L., *gets clothes from spinet.*) I don't know what I mean.

CARRIE. Go to Europe. What are you talking about? What's going to happen when trouble comes if we're not here to take care of it?

ANNA. (*At valise, packing.*) Why do you think trouble will come?

CARRIE. Because it always has. You know very well what I mean. Well, you go to Europe and I'll go to work.

ANNA. (*Laughs.*) All right.

CARRIE. (*In door.*) If Mr. Samuel Barrett has seen Julian's letter, I'll apologize. Mr. Barrett likes people to apologize. Nineteen years of faithful work matter for something. (*Giggles.*) Ho, ho. I'd like to see you in Europe alone.

(LILY *appears from the bedroom. She has on a skirt and over the skirt she has on a nightgown. She looks fogged and vague and she stares at* CARRIE *and* ANNA *as if she didn't know who they were.*)

ANNA. Morning. Julian want his breakfast?

LILY. I don't know. (*She points off* U. L. C.) He slept in there.

CARRIE. Mama and Papa's room.

LILY. (*Crosses* D. C.) He thought I was asleep when he went in there, but I wasn't.

CARRIE. No, you certainly weren't. You moved around most of the night. Are you dressed or undressed? Well, I'm off to work.

LILY. (*Sits ottoman.*) My. It's awfully hot to go to work.

CARRIE. Yes. And sometimes it's awfully cold.

(*She exits toward porch. As she moves out,* MRS. PRINE *appears in the garden.* HENRY *stands outside the garden fence. During the scene between* LILY *and* ALBERTINE *he will occasionally be seen moving back and forth.*)

MRS. PRINE. (*In gate.*) Good morning.

CARRIE. Good morning.

(*She hurries off. At the sound of her mother's voice,* LILY *runs to the porch, stares at her* MOTHER, *runs back in the room.*)

LILY. Oh. Where are my shoes? (*Stares down at herself, sees she is barefoot, hesitates.*) Oh. (*Runs out again to the porch and down to the garden.* ANNA *exits* D. L.) Mama. I don't know why I did that.

ALBERTINE. (*Moves toward her and they kiss.*) I come calling much too early. I forget that other people sleep at night.

LILY. I didn't.

ALBERTINE. I know.

LILY. (*Crosses to porch.*) What did Henry tell you?

ALBERTINE. That you were out, er, visiting, and wanted to speak with me.

LILY. Yes. I didn't want Henry to come and get me. I didn't need his help.

ALBERTINE. He said the neighborhood worried him at two o'clock in the morning.

38

LILY. (*Crosses to yard* L.) How did he know where I was?

ALBERTINE. You told him on the phone.

LILY. Did I? I don't remember—I was mean to Henry. Did he tell you that?

ALBERTINE. No.

LILY. (*After a second, crosses to her.*) I'm sorry I spoke that way.

ALBERTINE. How are you, Lily? I haven't seen you in a whole year. The garden wing of the house is being cleaned for you. You are very welcome, and I've come to say that to Julian.

LILY. Thank you. It's nice that you want us. Do you?

ALBERTINE. You are thinner, Lily. Have you been well?

LILY. Do you?

ALBERTINE. Do I what?

LILY. Do you really want me to come home again?

ALBERTINE. I'll come later. You must be tired from your—night's exercises. (*Turns to leave.*)

LILY. (*Quickly.*) Mama, don't go. Please. (*Crosses to* R. *of her.*) I need help. Your help. I'll start at the start and try not to take long and say things nice and clear—

ALBERTINE. There's no need. Don't distress yourself. I've guessed your trouble and I've brought you a check. (*She takes a check from her bag and puts it on the table.*) Will you and Julian come and dine at eight? Then you'll decide if you wish to move in, or if, in this heat, you prefer the lake house. I've always meant to give you the lake house, Lily, and tomorrow we'll go around and have Warkins do the papers. (*When there is no answer.*) At eight?

LILY. What does Mrs. Warkins look like? Does she speak in a low voice?

ALBERTINE. I don't know. I haven't seen her in years, and then only once or twice.

LILY. (*Crosses to porch.*) You haven't seen anybody in years, except Henry, of course. How old is Mrs. Warkins?

ALBERTINE. I know little about her, Lily. It's bad enough to know Warkins. I remember her as a tall woman with a sad face. Possibly from being married to a lawyer.

LILY. (*Crosses to* L. *of her.*) Is she in love with Mr. Warkins?

ALBERTINE. (*Smiles, shrugs.*) That is a remarkable idea. Thank God I've never been in a position to find out. Let's waste our time saying things like each to his own taste, and shaking our heads in gossip, but let's do it another time.

LILY. (*Crosses to* R. *of her.*) Please don't smile and shrug, Mama. It always makes me nervous. You are angry because I was mean to Henry last night, and he told you.

ALBERTINE. He told me nothing.

LILY. *I was mean to Henry.* That was bad of me, wasn't it?

ALBERTINE. (*Wearily, softly.*) I don't know.

LILY. Well, tell him I'm sorry.

ALBERTINE. You have been saying you are sorry, in space, for many years.

LILY. You *are* angry now.

ALBERTINE. Oh, Lily.

LILY. I don't know what makes me speak so wrong. All I want is to tell you, and have you help me. But I get things out of order—Mama, I'm in trouble.

ALBERTINE. I know Julian lost the factory. Well, perhaps he doesn't belong in a large city. He'll find something here. In the meantime— (*She picks up the check and hands it to* LILY.)

LILY. What is it, Mama?

ALBERTINE. (*Slowly, too patiently.*) I told you. It's a check. A check is for money. (*Sits bench.*) Money. It's five thousand dollars. It's yours. Oblige me by not speaking of it again.

LILY. Don't be angry with me.

ALBERTINE. (*After a second.*) Oh, Lily. Something always happens between us.

LILY. If I could only speak in order, then I wouldn't—

ALBERTINE. Don't fret. Everybody talks too much, too many words, and gets them out of order.

LILY. (*Crosses to yard* C.) I know you think that. I

40

know you do. That's what makes it so hard. It's that you never talk much, and you look down on people who don't do it very well.

ALBERTINE. You said you were in trouble. Do you wish to tell me about it?

LILY. (*Sits* D. L.) You speak so severely, Mama.

ALBERTINE. Please, Lily, let us cease this talking about talking. Tell me or do not tell me.

LILY. (*Quickly, loudly.*) Mama, we're rich.

ALBERTINE. Who?

LILY. Julian.

ALBERTINE. When you say rich, do you mean *money* rich or spiritual rich, or moral rich or—?

LILY. You're teasing me. Money rich.

ALBERTINE. Well, isn't that nice? Julian didn't lose the factory?

LILY. Yes, he lost it. We got rich some other way. There were phone calls from a lady and Julian would talk so I couldn't understand, and then we came here, and it all has to do with the lady, I think, and something else—

ALBERTINE. (*Very quickly.*) Never mind. Never mind. (*Rises.*) He'll probably tell me. What good news, Lily. I must say I hadn't expected it. Forgive my bringing the check. How impertinent of me to take for granted that Julian needed it. Don't tell him, just tear it up. Tonight we'll have a celebration—if I still know how. Shall we dine at Gallatoire's? (*When there is no answer, she stares at* LILY, *who is tearing the check.*) What trouble are you in?

LILY. First we lived in a big hotel in Chicago, and I didn't like it, and didn't have anything to do. Then we moved to a little, poor hotel and I learned to cook in the bathroom, and Julian and I were close together, and he didn't have his friends any more, and he was sad and sweet and often he stayed with me all day, in bed, and we'd read or sleep, and he'd tell me about things. We were never really hungry, but I'd have to watch the meat and give him my share when he wasn't looking because he likes meat, and I was very happy.

ALBERTINE. (D. R.) How often the rich like to play

41

at being poor. A rather nasty game, I've always thought. You had only to write me.

LILY. (*Rises, crosses to her.*) It wasn't a game, it wasn't. It was just after he lost all his money in the factory—

ALBERTINE. (*Looks at* LILY.) *Your* money in the factory. You like being poor and you're not going to be. Is that the trouble you are in? I can't be sorry for you, Lily. I don't think Julian would have liked the meat game for very long; and neither would you if the shortage had lasted much longer. (*Laughs, sitting bench.*) Cheer up. Good fortune isn't as bad as it seems.

LILY. You're laughing at me, and you shouldn't. Julian will leave me now.

ALBERTINE. Why?

LILY. (*Crosses to her.*) He is different. Things have changed.

ALBERTINE. Marriages change from day to day and year to year. All relations between people. Women, of course, have regrets for certain delicate early minutes, but— There is no answer to that.

LILY. Did you, Mama? Did you have those regrets?

ALBERTINE. I don't remember. I don't think so. Your father and I had very little together. And so we had little to regret.

LILY. I don't mean my father.

ALBERTINE. (*After a long silence.*) I came here because you were in trouble, or so you said. Not because I am. When I come to you for that reason, feel free to say what you wish. Until then, please do not.

LILY. Julian couldn't have me last night, and when I cried he said please not to, that— (*Crosses to porch.*) And so I went out and walked and walked. I had never seen that street before. I heard noise way up, and I went in. There were people and a woman stood before them on a box. The people talked about themselves right out loud. One woman had lost a leg but she said it was growing back and she proved it.

ALBERTINE. My goodness. (LILY *pauses.*) Are you dozing off?

42

LILY. And the lady on the box kept saying, "Truth, truth is the way to life, and the one way, the only way. Open your hearts with this knife and throw them here." (*Throws up her arms.*) She had a knife in her hand—

ALBERTINE. Do sit down, Lily.

LILY. And she kissed the knife— (*She kisses her hand in imitation.*)

ALBERTINE. Strange tastes people have. Don't kiss your own hand again, please.

LILY. (*Speaks quietly.*) Everybody left and there I was. The woman said, "You want me, child?" And I said, "Could I buy your knife?" "No," she said. "The knife is not for sale." But I wanted it more than I ever wanted anything and, well, (*Smiles, slyly.*) finally, we swapped something— And when it was in my hand, for the first time in my life, I just said everything, and asked. The lady said the knife of truth would dress me as in a jacket of iron flowers and though I would do battle, I would march from the battle cleansed. Then I fell asleep.

ALBERTINE. Your many religious experiences have always made me uneasy, Lily—

LILY. (*Crosses to her.*) When I woke up I knew that I must begin my struggle up the mountain path of truth by asking you—

ALBERTINE. You telephoned at two this morning to speak with me about a journey up a mountain path of truth?

LILY. And Henry came instead, and made me get in the car, and brought me *here.* He stood in the way— But he can't. Because I must ask truth, and speak truth, and act with truth, now and forever.

ALBERTINE. Do you think this is the proper climate? So hot and damp. Puts mildew on the truth.

LILY. Did you sell me to Julian, Mama? (ALBERTINE *rises, comes to* LILY, *stares at her, takes her by the shoulders.*)

ALBERTINE. (*Softly.*) Lily, take hold of yourself. Take hold.

LILY. Answer me.

ALBERTINE. You are my child, but I will not take much more of this.

LILY. (*In a cry.*) Mama, Mama, I didn't mean to hurt you. (*Puts her hand on her chest.*) But it's so bad for for me. Julian may leave me now, and he's all I ever had, or will, or want—Mama, did he marry me for money?

ALBERTINE. He married you because he loved you. Shame on you, Lily. You are looking for pain, and that makes me sad and always has.

LILY. I told you there is another woman. I saw them. I followed them and they went places where people wouldn't see them and they talked. And she has something to do with his getting rich.

ALBERTINE. Do you intend him never to speak to another woman? I don't know what you are talking about, getting rich, but it's good for people to have money of their own. The day comes when they don't like taking it from others. I know people thought of Julian as a charming man who didn't care about such things. But I never thought so.

LILY. Last night when I lay waiting for him, and he knew it, he said he'd had too much champagne and he wanted to sleep alone. It's been like that since the lady came to Chicago.

ALBERTINE. You've learned women's chit-chat very fast. I'm not good at this, but since we've started I can tell you that everybody wants to sleep alone sometimes, (*Laughs.*) maybe most of the time.

LILY. He liked to come to bed with me. You didn't know that, did you?

ALBERTINE. I have not read it in the newspaper. But, as you know, I'm a large stockholder, and if you'd like it reported in detail— (*She breaks off, puts her hand over her eyes, sits bench.*) Forgive me.

LILY. You'd never have believed anybody could want me. I didn't believe it, either. I was so scared at first that I— But there I was, good for the man I loved. He said I was better than anybody, and that I must learn to cook because he'd always believed that a woman who was good in the bedroom was good in the kitchen— (*She laughs happily. Softly.*) I was beloved, Mama, and I flourished. (*Sits table.*) Now I'm frightened. Help me.

ALBERTINE. (*Gently.*) How can I help you when I

don't understand what you're talking about? **Are you really saying** that if Julian stayed dependent on you, all would be safe, but if he has money for himself, and need not crawl to you—

LILY. That's an ugly way to speak, Mama.

ALBERTINE. On your struggle up the mountain path, you will find that truth is often ugly. It burns. (*After a second.*) I don't believe there is any other woman but in any case be wise enough to wait and find out.

LILY. (*Rises, crosses down* R. *of bench.*) I don't want to be wise, ever, Mama, ever. I'm in love.

ALBERTINE. Then be happy that Julian has finally had a little luck. Lily, he would have come to hate your money. *That* was the danger I feared for you.

LILY. I never wanted us to have money. I hate money. You know that, Mama.

ALBERTINE. Then be very careful. Same thing as loving it.

(*The phone rings and* LILY *wheels and makes a dash for the house. At the same minute,* ANNA, *who has been moving in and out of the room, packing the valise, now turns from the valise and crosses to the phone.* LILY *falls over the porch steps and rolls to the ground.* HENRY *crosses to porch, helps* LILY *rise.*)

LILY. Anna! Anna!

ALBERTINE. Lily.

ANNA. (*Into the phone.*) I will wake him. Just a minute. (*She moves out* U. L. C.)

LILY. (*Calling to* ANNA.) That's the woman. I want to speak to her. I want to ask her— (*She makes a sudden, violent movement up the porch steps.*)

ALBERTINE. No. (*Very sharply.*) No. (HENRY *touches* LILY'S *arm as if to keep her from moving.*)

LILY. (*To* HENRY.) Leave me alone. I told you that last night. (*Sits bench.*) I told it to you years ago when I rolled down the hill. I meant to roll down the hill and kill myself, but you didn't know it.

HENRY. (*Crosses behind bench.*) I knew it.

JULIAN. (*Appears in the living room, from* U. L. C.,

45

dressed in a robe, envelope of money in his pocket, moves to phone. Sits arm of R. *chair.*) Hello. Sorry about the call last night. I was dying to tell you the good news, but of course I couldn't call you back. Did the cough medicine work? Did you have a good night's sleep? This is the great day, so stop worrying. Everything went fine. Got it right here in my pocket, nice clean bills. Eleven o'clock, waving a fortune at you. Where we agreed. (*He listens, smiling.*) I did everything the way you told me, only better. Don't worry about me. He just beats women. (*Gently, affectionately.*) I'll be there. Good-bye, my dear. (ANNA *enters the living room from* D. L., *carrying a glass of juice and a dress.* JULIAN *takes juice from* ANNA, *kisses her.*) What's good for breakfast?

ANNA. Pancakes?

JULIAN. (*Looks around at the old dress she is packing.*) Why are you taking all that old stuff? Throw out everything old. (*Stares at* ANNA, *crossing to* L. *of her.*) What's the matter with you? You look terrible.

ALBERTINE. (*Through the window.*) Morning, Julian.

(ANNA *exits toward kitchen.*)

JULIAN. (*Gets mantilla box from piano and crosses to her on porch.*) Well, look who's here. Hello. A present for you.

ALBERTINE. Thank you.

(JULIAN *kisses her cheek, crosses toward* HENRY. ANNA *finishes packing, places valise below piano, exits to kitchen.*)

JULIAN. (*To* LILY.) Hello, darling. (*Stares at her.*) What's the matter with you? (LILY *shakes her head. He crosses to* HENRY *and they shake hands.* ALBERTINE *sits* D. L. *in yard.*) How's the fishing? Been up the bayou?

HENRY. Been up. But nobody got anything. Except crayfish.

JULIAN. Anybody asked what I missed most in Chicago, I'd have said a bayou, a bowl of crayfish, a good gun for a flight of wild ducks coming over— Going to buy a little place up there, first thing. You're welcome all the time. (*Sees that* LILY *has not moved and is staring at the ground.*) What's the matter, Lily? (*When she doesn't answer; he speaks to* ALBERTINE.) I sure manage to depress my ladies. Never used to be that way. Do I depress you?

ALBERTINE. (*Laughs.*) I'm very glad to see you.

(*She has now unwrapped the package and taken out a flame-red lace mantilla supported by a giant comb. She laughs as she arranges it on her head.*)

JULIAN. What's it meant for?

ALBERTINE. I don't know.

JULIAN. When do you wear it?

ALBERTINE. I'll wear it for reading in bed. How very nice of you to bring it to me.

JULIAN. (*As if the tone of thanks puzzled him.*) How nice of *you.* You put it on. Nobody else— (*Turns to* LILY.) Lily, did you show your Mama your new ring? (LILY *shakes her head.*) Oh. Go and get your ring and show your Mama. (LILY *hesitates and then moves inside, exits* U. R. C. *He smiles ruefully at* ALBERTINE, *points to mantilla.*) Silly present, isn't it? It cost a lot.

ALBERTINE. (*Laughs.*) Nice to buy, nice to get, silly presents. (*Puts mantilla in box.*) Who wants a roast of beef?

JULIAN. (*Smiles with pleasure.*) That's what I thought— (*Confidentially, points inside.*) I think I bought, got, brought— Well, they're sort of upset and they don't think I know it. I should have had sense enough to know that when you've been poor and wanted things you couldn't have, your stomach gets small and you can't eat much right away. I brought too much, and everything too grand, and, well— Guess they got a little sick. (*Sits table.*) They're so happy that it comes out unhappy. You know how it is?

ALBERTINE. I don't think so.

JULIAN. It's a crazy old world. For years, they (*Points inside.*) tell me about what's going to be, what I'm going to do, you know, get rich and big time. The more I fail, the louder they cheer me with what we're all going to have, want. And so all my life I dream about coming up those steps carrying everything, and I make up what they will say, and what I will say— (*Smiles.*) Well, when it came, I guess it (*Rises.*) was hard to believe, maybe even frightened them, I never thought of that, and I just bought anything if it cost a lot, and made Carrie sick on caviar, and everybody acted scared, and like they were going to cry. Lily did cry— Natural enough. You know?

ALBERTINE. (*Carefully.*) No, I don't know. You've had good fortune and brought it home. There's something sad in not liking what you want when you get it. And something strange, maybe even mean. (*Sharply, as if in warning.*) Nobody should have cried about your good fortune, nobody should have been anything but happy.

JULIAN. (*Moving about.*) No, no. You don't understand. They're happy. They just haven't had time— I scared them, Europe and a house and fancy things all in a day. Who wouldn't be scared? They thought I'd come home broke— God knows I always had—you don't know about that, but *they* do, and they got ready to give me all they had, and tell all the same, nice lies about how the next time. And then there I come, strutting like a kid— (*Laughs with great pleasure.*) Rich. Rich. Rich. (*As a child would say it. Goes to table, sits opposite her.*) I'm as good as you now. Isn't that true?

ALBERTINE. (*Laughs.*) I'm not sure.

JULIAN. We'll have to have long talks and consultations.

ALBERTINE. About money? I don't think so. I like it very much. But it makes dull talk.

JULIAN. Oh, I just bet you don't really think that. (*He pokes her with his finger; she stares at him and sits very straight.*) That's just the way *you* people want *us* to think. Not dull at all. Why, I had more fun this week— Know what I did? (*He pokes her again. She reacts sharply and* HENRY *laughs. She turns to look at* HENRY *and then turns back to* JULIAN, *smiling.*)

48

ALBERTINE. Henry doesn't like people to poke me, do you, Henry?

HENRY. I never saw anybody do it before.

JULIAN. I went to see a man I hated the two times I ever saw him and the many times I heard about him. Once when he teased me as a boy, and once when he made fun of me as a man. (*He stops, remembers, sighs.*) I guess he's the only man I ever hated. Well, I went right in his office and said I got something you want, and I'll take a hundred and fifty thousand dollars for it. After he said all about being crazy, and to get the hell out, he said, "Get your money from women—your sisters or your wife. You married her for it—" (*He speaks softly to* ALBERTINE.) Did people think that? Did they?

ALBERTINE. I don't see people. I never thought it.

JULIAN. (*Leans down, kisses her hand.*) Maybe I'll knock you down later, I said to him, but right now let's keep our minds on a hundred and fifty thousand dollars delivered a week from today. (*To* ALBERTINE.) Want to see? (*He takes the envelope from his pocket, holds it open for her.*)

ALBERTINE. (*Laughs.*) It does look nice. I don't think I ever saw anything larger than a hundred dollar bill.

JULIAN. I tell you, the rich don't have any fun with money.

ALBERTINE. Smells rather nice, too.

JULIAN. I put a little cologne water on it. (*As he puts the envelope back in his pocket.*) One hundred and fifty thousand dollars. (*Pokes her.*) Do people like you think it's a lot of money?

ALBERTINE. It's money. (*Very deliberately pokes him.*) People like me think it's a good beginning. It's not a great fortune, but if you want one it will start you off.

JULIAN. You know, I think so, too. (*Smiles at her, rising.*) Isn't it funny? I liked you, but I never talked easy with you before. Now you just seem to me like anybody else.

ALBERTINE. I'm sorry.

JULIAN. (*Leans over and kisses her cheek.*) I didn't mean it quite like that. I just mean that you always scared me, and now you don't. I guess most people like

49

you scared me. (*Smiles.*) I was kind of, well, kind of broken. I knew it, but I showed off to keep— (*He points inside.*)—them from— (*He turns to* HENRY.) It's bad for a man to feel gone. (*Then, very gaily.*) Like a miracle. I go in to see this bastard shaking, and I come out knowing I did fine, knowing I'm going to be all right forever. You understand it wasn't just the money?

ALBERTINE. (*Laughs.*) I don't understand very much. Why don't you wait and tell me when you can?

JULIAN. (*Sits table.*) All I mean, you do something right. *Just right.* You know a man's got to have what you've got—very different from trying to get a job or selling something he don't want. I just sat there calm and smiling until he got through trying to find out how I, *I,* bought two acres of swamp land before he did, and how I could know how much he needed it. I thought to myself, so this is the way the big boys do it, you poor fool for being so scared all your life. So I said, "Get through, will you, I got a board of directors meeting and have no more time for you." (*Laughs with pleasure.*) I don't know where I got that from. Maybe the movies. "You and my lawyer can attend to the rest, so agree or don't agree. I don't want to be in the room with you too long." He got white but he didn't say anything, so I got up and started out and he said, "All right. Give us two weeks to draw the papers—" My lawyer said, "Fair enough, sir," and I guess it was the "sir" that made me angry because I said, "No. I'll take it next Tuesday at two o'clock. Have it ready." And I walked out the happiest man in town. I paid back my life some way or other— (GUS *appears at gate carrying ice.*) You can lose for just so long— When you win, everything on you grows bigger, know what I mean? (*He laughs, pokes* ALBERTINE.)

ALBERTINE. (*Gives mantilla box to* HENRY.) And I grow black and blue. (*Crosses and sits bench.*)

GUS. (*Crossing to* R. *end porch steps.*) Hi. Home to stay?

JULIAN. (*Crosses and shakes his hand.*) Gus, just look at that new icebox. (GUS *crosses to screen door, stares*

50

in through the porch door.) Bought it more for you than for them.

GUS. In Chicago they keep it in the parlor?

JULIAN. (R. *of* GUS *on porch.*) Gus, my old friend Gus. You're going to have that farm, kid. Go find it and start with this. (*Hands him several large bills.* GUS *looks at them, but doesn't take them.*)

GUS. You at that again?

JULIAN. This time I made it. Throw the ice away—

GUS. Julian, I don't want that kind of trouble again.

JULIAN. Nobody'll come for it this time. I'm telling you the truth. (*Forces money on him.*) And there's as much more as you want. Now get going and find the farm.

GUS. (*Crosses* R.) Who the hell wants a farm? Got enough trouble. Where'd you make up the farm from? (*He goes around the garden and disappears* U. R.)

JULIAN. He said since we were kids about a farm— People talk about what they want, and then— How's that?

ALBERTINE. I guess most of us make up things we want, don't get them, and get too old, or too lazy, to make up new ones. Best not to disturb that, Julian. People don't want other people to guess they never knew what they wanted in the first place.

JULIAN. (*Crosses to yard* c.) That's real sad. I know what I want and *I'm* going to be happy getting it.

ALBERTINE. Well, I like nice, rich, happy relatives, although I never had any. But I have bad news for you, Julian—it's not simple being happy, and money doesn't seem to have much to do with it, although it has to do with other things more serious.

(CARRIE *comes in, moving slowly. She stops when she sees the* GROUP.)

JULIAN. Morning. Where you been?

CARRIE. (*Crossing to door.*) I—I've been downtown.

JULIAN. Buying things, I hope. (*To* ALBERTINE.) My sisters are going to Europe tomorrow. Isn't that fine, after years of—

51

CARRIE. Your sisters are not— (*Then softer.*) Come inside, please.

JULIAN. What's the matter?

CARRIE. (*Starts toward steps, sharply.*) Come inside.

JULIAN. (*Playfully, but with meaning, crossing to her.*) Carrie, stop talking like that. You got a new man on your hands. You got to talk to me different now, like I'm a tycoon. (*To* ALBERTINE.) What's a tycoon? How much, I mean?

ALBERTINE. Miss Carrie can tell you. She works for one.

JULIAN. Barrett? Is he? I don't want to be like Barrett—

CARRIE. He knows what you think of him. He'd already read your letter when I got there. I can't tell you what I felt. All I could think to say was that it was a joke and you'd be down later to apologize.

JULIAN. (*After a second.*) Did you? Did you really say that? Don't ever say that again, Carrie. That's one of the things I don't ever have to do any more. That's one of the things money's going to buy us all.

CARRIE. I want to see you alone, Julian.

JULIAN. I don't think you should have gone to see him at all. We'll talk about it another time. I'm busy today. (*She wheels around, angry.* JULIAN *is grinning at* ALBERTINE.) How you like me? See? Got no time for small matters.

CARRIE. Small matters? After nineteen years. He said he didn't believe you wrote the letter. He said I wrote it, that it was like me, that he always had known about— (*She gasps.*) things in me. After nineteen years of loyalty—I want you to get dressed and go tell him that if you owe him an apology, he owes me an apology for the awful words he said—

JULIAN. (*To* ALBERTINE.) That's how tycoons act toward loyal ladies?

ALBERTINE. I don't know how they act toward loyal ladies.

CARRIE. (*Crossing inside.*) Julian— (*Sits* D. L.)

ALBERTINE. I do know tycoons are not romantic about money.

52

JULIAN. Ah, can't I be romantic for a month?

ALBERTINE. All right. We'll give you a month. Right now it's my impression that everybody around here thinks you held up a bank.

JULIAN. No, a poker game. Or a jewel robbery. (*Crossing to* U. R. *window.*) Hey, Lily. Lily! Come and show your Mama your ring. Lily! (*To* ALBERTINE.) *You* don't think I stole the money, do you? (*He looks at his watch, moves quickly into parlor as* LILY *appears.*)

ALBERTINE. (*Because* JULIAN *is going into the house, and because she speaks very softly, he does not hear her.*) No. I think I know where you got it.

JULIAN. (*As he passes* LILY, *he picks up her left hand.*) Go show your Mama— Where's your ring?

LILY. Somewhere.

JULIAN. Where is somewhere?

LILY. (*Crossing to porch.*) Don't be angry, please—

JULIAN. Why not? (*He sees* CARRIE.) Seen a large diamond ring?

CARRIE. Up to yesterday we never had such problems. How does one look for a diamond ring? Julian, he said bad things to me. Julian. (*He doesn't answer, starts to leave the room.*) Julian. Please answer me.

JULIAN. (U. C.) Answer you what?

CARRIE. Once, and not long ago, you'd have known by my face, and you'd have kissed me and said, "What is it, my Carrie?" (*Behind* CARRIE, ANNA *appears from* D. L., *carrying a breakfast tray. She stops.*)

JULIAN. (*Gently, crossing to her.*) What is it, my Carrie?

CARRIE. I want to talk to you— Let's go by ourselves, the way we used to—

JULIAN. I'm due downtown—

CARRIE. You have no time for me. We're coming apart, you and I—

JULIAN. What are you talking about?

CARRIE. You've come home in all this mystery, and not said a word with me alone—

JULIAN. (*Crossing* U. C.) When I take you to the boat tomorrow, I'll tell you all about "this mystery—"

CARRIE. (*Rises.*) I want to speak to you now. Now.

JULIAN. (*Softly, crossing to her.*) Did you always use that tone with me? Did you? (*To* ANNA.) Did you? (*When she doesn't answer.*) Say something, so I can tell the way you talk to me.

ANNA. Breakfast.

JULIAN. (*Takes the tray from her.*) Will you press a shirt for me? (*She nods and moves off with him.*)

CARRIE. You're saying no to me, when I need you?

JULIAN. I'm not saying no to you. I'm saying that I'm in a hurry. (*He exits* U. R. C.)

ALBERTINE. (*To* LILY, *who is on the porch.*) What did you do with the ring?

LILY. I don't want it.

ALBERTINE. He will be hurt. I suggest that you pretend that you do want it. (*Crosses to her.*)

LILY. (*Crosses and sits* D. L.) I don't want it.

(CARRIE, *nervously moving about, comes to stand at the window and to listen to the voices in the garden.*)

ALBERTINE. There are many ways of loving. I'm sure yours must be among them. Put white flowers in your hair, walk up your mountain of truth with a white banner in your hand—and as you drop it on his head, speak of love.

LILY. I gave her the ring and she gave me the knife.

ALBERTINE. I beg your pardon?

HENRY. (*Quickly.*) I know what she means.

LILY. I gave the lady the ring and she gave me the knife. I didn't want the ring, and I didn't know Julian would care. But I will go and tell him the truth now and— (*She starts into the room.*)

ALBERTINE. (*Stops her on porch step.*) You asked my advice and here it is: you do too much. Go and do nothing for a while. Nothing. I have seen you like this before: (*With force.*) I tell you now, do nothing. (*To* HENRY.) You know the address of the upstairs knife lady?

LILY. Mama, don't make fun—of her.

ALBERTINE. No, indeed. We will try to find your ring. Decide whether your costume is meant for day or night,

54

and rest yourself. (*Softly.*) Lily, don't tell Julian about the ring. (LILY *nods, enters the house. She sees* CARRIE, *smiles at her and exits toward the kitchen.* ANNA *appears carrying a shirt and crosses the room toward the kitchen. On porch.*) Well, there it is.

HENRY. You are not wise with Lily.

ALBERTINE. No. I never was. Well, it's been a good year, hasn't it? The best I ever had.

HENRY. Nothing has happened.

ALBERTINE. I know Lily. You do, too.

HENRY. She is jealous and scared—

ALBERTINE. And nothing I say will stop her from being foolish. (*Crosses and sits bench.*) And of course there is another woman. But Julian isn't sleeping with her. (*Laughs.*) They raised him to be a very, very moral man.

HENRY. Very, very moral men sometimes sleep with women. I think.

ALBERTINE. But it shows on them. Do you think he's sleeping with another woman?

HENRY. He's not sleeping with her, and he won't. But he used to.

ALBERTINE. Yes? (*When there is no answer.*) Cy Warkins is the man he's talking about, Cy Warkins who bought what he calls his two acres of swamp land. I'm not sure why Cy wanted it so much, but if it's down by the river I can make a good guess. Warkins owns fifty percent of the stock of the interstate agreement to take the railroad route along the docks. (*Laughs.*) If my guess is right, he must have been surprised that Julian knew about the best kept secret in years. I regret not being there when Julian told him. But who told Julian? Mrs. Warkins? (HENRY *does not answer.*) She never liked Warkins and that was the only thing I ever knew about her. But she must be forty now. (*When there is no answer.*) But of course she wasn't always forty. (*She points inside.*) They knew each other? And she told him about the railroad? I'm not gossiping, you know that.

HENRY. I think that's what happened. She was in love with Julian once. She hates Warkins and has wanted to leave for years. Maybe this is the money to leave with.

ALBERTINE. (*Softly, in a new tone; as if it were forced out of her, and she was ashamed.*) How do you know about Mrs. Warkins? Please.

HENRY. I don't know about her any more, but I used to. She's a cousin to me.

ALBERTINE. (*Stares at him, and then laughs.*) She's part colored? Isn't that wonderful! Did Warkins know when he married her?

HENRY. He doesn't know now. But Julian did, and didn't care. She's a foolish woman and grateful for such things.

ALBERTINE. That's understandable, God knows.

HENRY. Not to me. I am not grateful, nor ungrateful, nor any word like that.

ALBERTINE. Nor should you be. You are in a bad humor with me this morning. You are disapproving. What have I done or said?

HENRY. (*Softly.*) You look tired.

ALBERTINE. (*Rises, goes to him.*) The world has many people who make many things too hard for too little reason, or none at all, or the pleasure, or stupidity. We've never done that, you and I.

HENRY. Yes, we've done it. But we've tried not to.

(ALBERTINE *touches his hand.* HENRY *smiles and puts her hand to his face.* ALBERTINE *turns and, as she does, she sees* CARRIE *in the window. She pauses, as if to ask herself what* CARRIE *could have heard.*)

ALBERTINE. Are you writing a book, Miss Carrie?

CARRIE. (*Softly.*) This is our house, Mrs. Prine.

ALBERTINE. (*Sighs.*) Indeed.

(HENRY *takes her arm and they move off.* LILY *comes running into the room, holding her right hand in her left hand. She is followed by* ANNA *who carries a bottle and gauze bandage.* LILY *runs toward the hall, calling out:*)

LILY. Julian, I—I cut my hand.

ANNA. Lily.

56

LILY. Julian. I cut my hand. (*Then she turns and going to screendoor, calls out loudly toward the garden.*) Mama. Mama. I cut my hand.

CARRIE. Your Mama has left with her friend.

JULIAN. (*Appears* U. R. C. *with shaving soap on face.*) What's the matter?

LILY. I cut my hand.

JULIAN. (*Seats* LILY *on ottoman, kneels* R. *of her. Picks up* LILY's *hand, holds it for* ANNA *to apply pad with antiseptic.*) It's a deep one. You ought not to have rusty knives in the kitchen.

(ANNA *looks up as if about to speak, changes her mind, crosses to piano, puts down antiseptic bottle.*)

LILY. Ouch. (*She holds out her hand to* JULIAN. *He kisses it and she gently touches his face. She rubs her thigh.*) And last night I fell in here and hit my leg. You could cure that, too. Please. Make me cured, Julian. Let's go to bed and maybe you'll be pleased with me— Maybe. (*She puts his hand on her breast.* ANNA *turns away;* CARRIE *stands staring at them.*) And if you're pleased with me, then all the bad will go away, and I will pray for it to be that way. But if you're not, I'll understand, and won't ask why— (*She laughs gaily, slyly; presses his hand on her breast.*) But *if* you are pleased with me, darling— (JULIAN *leans down to kiss her.*) I have missed you. (*He picks her up in his arms and begins to move out of the room to* U. C.)

CARRIE. (*Sucks in her breath; enters to doorway; loudly.*) I read in a French book that there was nothing so abandoned as a respectable young girl.

JULIAN. (*Laughs.*) That's true, thank God. (*He leans down to kiss* LILY's *hair.*) Otherwise nobody could stand them. (LILY *laughs merrily.*)

CARRIE. (*Comes toward them.*) You didn't fall in here last night. When I turned on the light—

LILY. Yes, ma'am. I fell. I didn't see the spinet— (JULIAN, *carrying* LILY, *exits* U. R. C.)

CARRIE. You did not fall against the spinet. You were on this side of the room, hitting—

ANNA. Carrie.

CARRIE. (L. *of table.*) She was hitting herself against that table. Just doing it. I saw her. I tell you, I saw her.

ANNA. I believe you.

CARRIE. (*Crossing to window.*) He doesn't know she went out last night. He doesn't know she gave her ring away—to some woman— She's told him lies. She lies to him, she tricks him. I think she's a crazy girl— (*Points to garden.*) And that woman knows it. I think there's a crazy girl in there—

ANNA. (C. *Softly, as if to herself.*) She cut her hand, quite deliberately and calmly, with a knife she took from a valise. She said a kind of prayer over the knife—

CARRIE. (*Moves swiftly toward* ANNA.) You saw her do that? You saw her cut herself? I tell you she's crazy. (*She moves toward door* U. C.)

ANNA. No.

CARRIE. (*Crosses to piano.*) How can you stand what's happening here? He comes home with all this money nonsense. He's married to a crazy girl. I think he's in bed with a girl—

ANNA. (*Crosses to her.*) He wanted. It's not our business.

CARRIE. It is our business that our brother has dealings with Mr. Cyrus Warkins, and Mr. Cyrus Warkins doesn't like them. Warkins is a powerful and dangerous man in this town, and Julian would be a baby in the hands of such a man—

ANNA. What are you talking about?

CARRIE. (*Back to window.*) I don't know all it means. (*Points out to garden.*) But I heard them say this money, or whatever, has to do with Warkins' wife.

ANNA. (D. C.) He slept with Charlotte Warkins ten years ago. It's been over that long.

CARRIE. How do you know such a thing? How do *you* know?

ANNA. Because he told me.

CARRIE. I don't believe you. You're a liar.

ANNA. Be quiet, Carrie.

CARRIE. You've made it up, you always made up things like that. It didn't happen. He would never have told *you.* He would have told me. He was closer to me–– There he is, another man, not our brother, lost to us after all the years of work and care, married to a crazy little whore who cuts her hand to try to get him into bed— (*Moves* U. C. ANNA *stops her and she swings around and back to window. Points to garden.*) The daughter of a woman who keeps a nigger fancy man. I'll bet she paid Julian to take that crazy girl away from her—

ANNA. (U. C.) Stop that talk. You know that's not true. Stop talking about Julian that way.

CARRIE. Let's go and ask him. Let's go and ask your darling child. (*Crosses* U. C. ANNA *stops her and pushes her back.*) Your favorite child, the child you made me work for, the child I lost my youth for— You used to tell us that when you love, truly love, you take your chances on being hated by speaking out the truth. (*Points inside.*) Go in and do it.

ANNA. All right. I'll take that chance now. Don't you know what's the matter, don't you know? You want him and always have. Years ago I used to be frightened and I would watch you and suffer for you.

CARRIE. (*Crosses to porch. After a second, in a whisper.*) You never said those words. Tell me I never heard those words. Tell me, Anna. (*When there is no answer.*) You were all I ever had. I don't love you any more.

ANNA. That was the chance I took.

CURTAIN

59

ACT THREE

Shortly after. Carrie *is pacing slowly in the parlor.*
Anna *enters* U. L. *with bag.* Carrie *crosses to porch
as* Anna *puts bag below piano and exits* D. L. *Offstage there is the sound of a BANJO and* Julian's
voice. He enters U. R., *crosses to window seat and
sings through window to* Carrie.

Julian. (*Dressed in trousers and undershirt. He
smiles, pleasantly at* Carrie.)*
>This is the big day, this is the great day
>This is the Bernier day.
>Never been one, No, never, never,
>Never been such a Bernier day.
>Never been such a day before.
>Going to be more and plenty more.
>Oh, it's money day, the end of trouble day,
>And going to be more and plenty more.
>Never been such a day before.
>Not for Mama, Not for Papa,
>Not for sister, Not for Brother—
>Going to be more and plenty more.
>>(*Shouts off.*)

Anna! Where's my shirt?

Carrie. (*Softly, through window.*) Do you know that
all I want in this world is what will be good for you?

Julian. And I for you. (Anna *appears carrying his
shirt. Places it on back of* L. *chair. Exits* U. R. C.)
>Now every day she going to be
>She going to be a Bernier day.
>Say every day she going to be
>She going to be a Bernier day,
>And for Mama, and for Papa
>And for sister and for brother
>Going to be just a Bernier day.

**See back of book for music.*

60

(ANNA *returns to above* L. *chair with coat and tie; sits arm of* R. *chair. To* ANNA.)

It's the best day of my life since I won the bag of marbles from old Gus. You made me give them back. You said he was a poor colored boy. But I was a poor white boy, so I didn't know what you were getting so fancy about. Well, I'm on my way to the best day. (*To* CARRIE, *pointing to valise.*) Getting packed? Getting excited?

CARRIE. I'll practice today and tonight I'll give a little concert for you and we'll sing all the pieces you used to like.

JULIAN. Er. We'll be leaving today. We'll be going. (*Nervously.*) And *you'll* be leaving tomorrow, so just one day— Course I'll wait until tomorrow if you need me—

CARRIE. Where are you going?

JULIAN. Maybe a camping trip, maybe New York--

CARRIE. A few weeks?

JULIAN. (*Crosses and puts banjo on piano. Puts on shirt.*) I don't know. No. A year or so. And then back here, of course. This is where I belong. Where I want to be, where I was meant to be. (*Over-cheerful.*) And by that time you world travellers will be back and—

CARRIE. *You* want to go? Or *Lily* wants to go?

JULIAN. Never seen New York, either of us.

CARRIE. Lily wants to go.

JULIAN. I don't know. I just decided. We'll come back, don't worry, and— (*He takes out bank-book from hip pocket.*)

CARRIE. Why did you suddenly decide to go? Why?

JULIAN. (*Holds up bank-book.*) Some people got a family bible. We got a savings bank-book. (*Softly to* CARRIE.) Don't look like that. (*Points inside.*) She's young and—I don't think she wanted to come back. I didn't think about it before but— And maybe we should be alone for a while. That's all. (*Points to book.*) Twenty thousand going in here this morning. Twenty thousand dollars. That going to be enough? (*Laughs with pleasure.*) For six months maybe? Enough?

61

ANNA. I don't know anything about twenty thousand dollars.

JULIAN. (*Takes tie from her, puts it on, crossing* D. L.) You got to learn fast. Fast, I say. What was that word Mama used to use?

CARRIE. (*In a cry as she enters screen door, hold at door.*) Julian, don't go—

ANNA. (*Very fast.*) Faner. Elle commence a se faner. The leaf came in the spring, stayed nice on the branch until the winds would come to blow it in the snow. Mama said that in the little time of holding on a woman had to make ready for the winter ground where she would lie the rest of her life. A leaf cannot rise from the ground and go back to the tree, remember that. I remembered it. But when it came there was nothing I could do.

JULIAN. (*Gently, touches her.*) Mama was mean.

CARRIE. (*Shrilly.*) Anna always says something about Mama when things are wrong. Always. Mama wasn't mean to you. Just to us.

JULIAN. (*Crosses to* C. ANNA *sits* R. *arm of* L. *chair.*) Did you think I liked it that way? Did you? Mama had a tough time, I guess. That often makes people mean. (*Softly to* ANNA.) You're still on the tree, still so nice and pretty, and when the wind does come, a long time from now, I'll be there to catch you with a blanket made of warm roses, and a parasol of dollar bills to keep off the snow. Dollar bills make a mighty nice parasol, I just bet you. (*Smiles.*) For another good lady, too. (*As if to himself, crossing to* D. L.) Well, I'm off to give them to her. I'll walk right down Sailor's Lane and she'll be waiting for me. I'll take her arm, we'll have a cup of coffee, and I'll try to say thank you. No, I won't. People are always saying thank you so they can forget what they said it for. (*Holds up one envelope.*) I'll just hand this to her and say, "Have a good life, baby," and then I'll walk her down to the depot and put her on the train. A happy day. (*Holds up other envelope.*) Then I'll go around and bank our share. That'll make me respectable, won't it?

ANNA. (*After a second.*) Is she fanée?

JULIAN. Yes. A long time ago.

ANNA. Then wish her well from me.

JULIAN. I will.

CARRIE. Is the lady going to New York?

JULIAN. I don't know where she's going. I guess so. Doesn't everybody go to New York? (LILY, *on the last of* CARRIE'S *speech, comes into the room from* U. R. C. JULIAN *turns and grins at her. Crosses to her* U. C. ANNA *crosses* D. L.) Want to go to New York, or a fishing trip to Canada, or the Grand Canyon, or— Today?

LILY. With you?

JULIAN. (*Crosses to her, holds her face with his hand.*) How would you like that? Time we found a place. Wherever.

LILY. You and me?

JULIAN. You and me.

LILY. And will the not happening, happen to us again?

JULIAN. (*Sharply.*) Lily, stop that. (*Leads her to porch.* CARRIE *crosses* U. C. *in parlor.*) I was tired and nervous the last few days and am now. Any man will tell you that happens. (*Then, smiling.*) Only you must never talk such things with any man, hear me?

LILY. (*Giggles.*) I won't. (*As they embrace, she drops the knife from her right hand. She looks down at it as if surprised.*)

JULIAN. (*Leans down, picks up the knife, stares at it.*) What in the name of God is this?

LILY. The knife of truth. Will you swear on it? Swear that you will keep me with you whatever—

JULIAN. (*Seats her on garden bench. Sits with her.*) Lily. What the hell's the matter with you? Stop talking foolish and stop playing with knives. Maybe kiddies should marry kiddies. But I'm thirty-four. Stop talking about last night and what didn't happen, because it's the kind of thing you don't talk about. Can't you understand that? (*Gently.*) Now go pack your bags and go tell your Mama we're going away. (*Crosses in to* ANNA *above* R. *chair. Puts on coat, which she has brought.*)

LILY. (*Laughing with pleasure, crosses to porch.*) Can I say we're going away forever? Just us.

JULIAN. Forever. Just us. (*Turns, sees* CARRIE *and* ANNA *and stops.*) I mean we'll come back here, or the folks will come to us— (*Very fast.*) You'll see. You'll come to visit us, we'll come to visit you— Buy us a little house up the bayou— Sometimes I wish I had gone on up the bayou years ago—

ANNA. You did.

JULIAN. (*He smiles at her.*) Maybe I should have stayed. They said I was better with a muskrat boat than any Cajun, better with a gun. A nice little shack and a muskrat boat, all the bob white you could ever want— (*After a second.*) Fine morning to be talking like this.

ANNA. (*Sharply to* JULIAN.) Go on. (*He crosses to porch.*)

LILY. (*She holds him; he puts his arms around her.*) Will you be coming back for me?

JULIAN. What? What are you talking about? (*He looks pleadingly at all of them.*) What's the matter? Please. It's the best day of my life. Please somebody look happy.

ANNA. Go on. (*He turns and kisses* LILY *and runs off. After a second,* LILY *sits down on garden bench as if she were very tired.* ANNA *speaks to* CARRIE.) I wanted to be around the children he will have. I wanted something nice to grow old for. I held on to that and prayed for it. (*Very softly.*) This time he will go forever.

CARRIE. I don't believe it. You must have your headaches again. He will not go forever, or even for long—

ANNA. This time I say he will go forever. You lusted and it showed. He doesn't know he saw it, but he did see it, and some day he'll know what he saw. (*With great violence.*) You know the way that happens? You understand something, and don't know that you do, and forget about it. But one night years ago I woke up and knew what I had seen in you, and always seen. It will happen that way with him. It has already begun.

CARRIE. I told you I didn't love you any more. Now I tell you that I hate you. We will have to find a way to live with that.

ANNA. I don't think so. (*She moves out to the porch on her way to the garden.* CARRIE *exits* D. L.)

LILY. Will he come back for me, Miss Anna?

ANNA. What's the matter with you, child? You must

64

go and dress and pack your things. Julian won't be long and he'll want you to be ready. Shall I call your mother?

LILY. She talked cold to me. (*She imitates her mother.*) Try not to excite yourself, Lily. Try to make yourself clear, Lily. But when she talks to Henry— (*In another voice; soft and gentle.*) "Lily has gone to bed. Sit down. What shall we read tonight?" (*In her own voice.*) And one night she said to him, "Oh, God, make the time when we can be alone; make it come before we are both too old to have pleasure from peace." (*Softly, crossing to foot of steps.*) She would have paid anything for that time. Did she? Did she pay Julian? Is that why he took me?

ANNA. (*Very sharply.*) How dare you speak that way of Julian? What a bitter thought about a man who loves you.

LILY. (*Crosses D. R.*) No. Who would want me for any other reason?

ANNA. Your modesty does not excuse you.

LILY. I love him, Miss Anna. If he said he loved somebody else— Well, I'd just go away and he'd be rid of me. But this way— I know you understand.

ANNA. A woman who marries a man she loves should have a little more happiness from it and talk a little more sense. That's all I understand.

LILY. I've upset you, Miss Anna.

ANNA. Yes. You're rather an expert.

(*She disappears around the garden, U. R. LILY crosses and sits on rocker. CARRIE enters D. L. with broom and piece of cardboard. She moves to the porch, leans broom against screen.*)

LILY. Cleaning day? (*CARRIE does not answer as she moves porch table to yard.*) Do you like to sweep? I like to mop.

CARRIE. Have you done much? Two or three times, say?

LILY. I'm sorry you don't like me. I wanted you to.

CARRIE. (*Indicating she wants to move rocker.*) I would like to sweep the porch. Would you—

LILY. (*Moves* D. R. CARRIE *places rocker* R. *in yard.*)
Last night, in bed, Julian was thinking, I watched him.
And thinking isn't the way to make love.

CARRIE. (*Returns for fern stand.*) I don't know much
about gentlemen in bed and I don't want to learn from
you.

LILY. Haven't you ever slept with a man?

CARRIE. (*Turns, stares at her.*) Shall we have a pillow
fight or make fudge? I don't like these girlish con-
fidences. (*Places fern stand* R.)

LILY. Oh, Miss Carrie. I wanted you to like me.

CARRIE. (*Gets sprinkling can, sprinkles porch.*) There
is no need to worry about me any more.

LILY. Oh, I do. And I will. I'm frightened of you.

CARRIE. (*Angrily.*) Your favorite word. Did it ever
occur to you that other people are frightened, too?

LILY. You? No. No, indeed. Of what, Miss Carrie?

CARRIE. (*Sweeps.*) Of my hair which isn't nice any
more, of my job, which isn't there any more, of praying
for small things and knowing just how small they are, of
walking by a mirror when I didn't know it would be
there— (*She gasps.*) People say, "Those Bernier girls,
so devoted. That Carrie was pretty, and then one day she
wasn't; just an old maid, working for her brother." They
are right. An old maid with candied oranges as a right
proper treat each Saturday night. We didn't see people
any more, I guess, because we were frightened of saying
or hearing more than we could stand. (*Very angrily.*)
There are lives that are shut and should stay shut, you
hear me, and people who should not talk about themselves, and that was us.

LILY. (R. *of steps.*) Why don't you come away with
us, Miss Carrie?

CARRIE. Stop sticking your baby-pins into me. Go
inside and pray that another woman won't do it to you.
I want to clean the porch.

LILY. (*Crossing to door.*) There is another woman.
I've seen her. Nobody believes me.

CARRIE. I believe you.

LILY. I don't know who she is. Do you?

66

CARRIE. Your mother knows. ASK her. (*Sweeps dirt onto cardboard.*)

LILY. (*Giggles.*) I just bet that's true. But Mama won't tell me because she doesn't like me and doesn't tell me things. (*Runs to* CARRIE.) You know what does the harm? I keep thinking that Mama paid Julian to marry me. And then sometimes I think that's not true; he does love me. God made him love me because God knew how much I needed him. (*Smiles, ingratiating.*) He just worships you, Miss Carrie, and I know he confides in you. Did he ever tell you Mama paid him? (*Grabs* CARRIE'S *arm and, in the force of the movement, throws* CARRIE *off balance.*) Tell me. Be good to me. Tell me.

CARRIE. (*Pulls away.*) I tell you what I think: you're going to drive him crazy. (*Starts to move off.* LILY *grabs her.*)

LILY. Did my Mama—

CARRIE. I don't know what she did. All he told us was that he had fallen in love and was going to be married.

LILY. (*In a transport of pleasure.*) Oh. (*Laughing with happiness.*) Miss Carrie! Miss Carrie! (*She pirouettes to* D. L. *and sits.*) He told you he was in love! Isn't that nice?

CARRIE. (*Replaces fern stand, table, rocker. Sits* R. *bench.*) I remember wondering why he had picked that Sunday to tell us. Anna was going to the hospital the next morning for her eye operation. None of us had never been in a hospital before, and we didn't know about the costs, and being in a ward, and all of that. So Julian came home and told about you, and then he said that Anna was going to have the best room in the hospital and he had called the great Dr. Kranz in Philadelphia, and the great Dr. Kranz was already on the train. He wouldn't let Anna say a word, said he won the money in a poker game. I don't know. Anna was more worried about that than about her eyes. And she fussed and fussed and never liked the fancy room and the uppity private nurses. But Dr. Kranz did a wonderful operation and when she came out of it, the first thing she said to Julian was, "My eyes were not made to make all this trouble for you." And he said a beautiful thing to her,

67

he said, "Look, I'd give my both arms and one leg for you, but not two legs, so maybe I don't love you as much as I think," and how we all laughed. (*She smiles at* LILY.) A few days later he brought you to see Anna. Do you remember?

LILY. (*Who has been staring at* CARRIE, *crosses on porch.*) Yes.

CARRIE. I was happy that Julian was to be married.

LILY. You said so. (*Very loudly, as if out of control.*) I didn't believe you.

CARRIE. Oh, I could have stopped the marriage, even you must have guessed that.

LILY. (*Kneels.*) Even I. But you didn't stop it because you knew my mother had paid Julian— I'm glad I helped Miss Anna, I really am—would go on paying him, and you didn't have to worry about a little girl who didn't mean anything more to anybody than a bank check.

CARRIE. I have said none of that. You have been looking for it, and you would have found it in anything I, or anybody else, could say.

LILY. I don't mind, not much. It's better to know. I will take Julian any way I can have him. *If* I can have him. I feel most bad and sad, Miss Carrie, because what he married me for, he doesn't need any more. Isn't that true?

CARRIE. (*Crosses to screen door, gets broom.*) I don't know. Take your questions to Mrs. Cyrus Warkins. She'll be in New York. You can have many a cozy evening.

LILY. She's coming with us?

CARRIE. (*Crosses* D. L. *in parlor.*) No. She's going on the morning train. (*Exits* D. L. *Leaves broom.*)

LILY. (*Follows to* C. *in parlor.*) I see. Is she a tall, dark lady?

CARRIE. (*Enters, gets fan* U. R. *sideboard; crosses to window.*) I've never seen her. But Henry is tall and dark and she's his cousin, so perhaps. Your mother was very amused that the great lawyer Warkins had married a part nigra and didn't know it.

LILY. Does Julian love her?

CARRIE. I used to think I knew about Julian. I didn't.

68

Ask your mother and her fancy man. They said Julian and the woman were together years ago. And my sister confirms the alliance.

LILY. (*Giggles too loudly, sits piano stool.*) Alliance? Alliance in bed? What a funny way to say it. Julian told me that you talked like an old maid when you were twelve years old, and that Gus used to say you kept your vagina in the icebox, that he'd seen it there and shut the door fast.

CARRIE. (*Very loudly.*) Stop that filthy talk. Julian never said a thing like that—

LILY. (*Crosses* C.) Oh, please, I didn't mean to offend you. Julian said it in fun. Afterwards in bed, we always talked fun. That's almost the best time, when you laugh and say things you'd never say anyplace else, and it's all in honor bright. (*Sits ottoman.*) It's then that you ask about other girls, everybody does, Julian told me, and every man thinks it's a big bore he's got to get through for the next time, if you know what I mean. (CARRIE *crosses* U. C.) Julian said there was only one woman that ever mattered, long ago, and I wasn't to worry— (*She laughs.*) and that she was married to a bastard who beat her, and if he ever made money he'd give it to her to get away. (*She smiles.*) So now she's coming with us. What will they do with me? (*She screams.*) It pains me. I can't tell you. I'll ask her not to come. I'll tell her I don't blame her, of course, and I'll swear on my knife of truth that if I have just one more year— (*Grabs the phone book, holds it out to* CARRIE.) Please find it for me.

CARRIE. Mrs. Warkins isn't home. She's waiting for Julian.

LILY. (*Runs toward the porch, leaving phone book on* C. *table.*) I'll run.

CARRIE. (*Sits* L. *chair.*) Put your clothes on first. You've got a long way to go in your underwear.

LILY. (*Stares down at her nightgown.*) Please you go, Miss Carrie. (*Crosses* C.)

CARRIE. Oh, I don't think so.

LILY. You don't talk the way you did. You talk real mean.

CARRIE. In the last day I lost my brother, my sister,

my job. That's all I had to lose. Perhaps it's the fear of losing people that make us talk nice or better. (*Very loudly, sharply.*) Don't you think? Don't you think maybe?

LILY. What time is Julian going to take her away?

CARRIE. (*Carefully.*) I did not say he was going to take her away. He has gone to meet Mrs. Warkins— evidently to give her a share.

LILY. (*Gets phone book and sits window seat.*) What time is it? I know Mr. Cyrus Warkins, he's Mama's lawyer. Mrs. Warkins is a sad lady, if she's the one who was on the train.

CARRIE. She's ailing, I've always heard, and doesn't go into society. But I suppose the real reason is that she's part nigra and thought somebody would find out. Julian didn't mind. Imagine that. He didn't mind.

LILY. Why should he? I don't mind Henry's being colored. I just hate Henry because he's Henry. (*There is a long pause; as if LILY had dozed.*)

CARRIE. (*Watching LILY, sighs, crossing U. C.*) Your mind wanders, doesn't it? Go pack your bags now.

LILY. (*Crossing to CARRIE with book.*) You're a fine lady. He'd listen to you. Miss Carrie, please call Mr. Cyrus Warkins.

CARRIE. I will not call Mr. Cyrus Warkins. His wife is not going to New York with me.

LILY. (*Runs to porch.*) Mama should call him. Where's Mama? She went for my ring. (*Re-enters and crosses to phone.*) Will Mr. Warkins listen to me? Nobody does. Don't you want to help me? It's hot, isn't it?

CARRIE. Wait for your Mama.

LILY. It will be too late.

CARRIE. I think so.

LILY. You're teasing me. It's not nice to tease me and to pretend that you're not. (*As CARRIE moves away.*) Miss Carrie, please.

CARRIE. (*Sharply.*) What do you want of me? What is it that you want?

LILY. I don't want to be in the room alone. (*Points down to telephone.*) It's for the best, the best for every-body, isn't it?

CARRIE. What's the sense of answering you? You just go on talking and talking.

LILY. No, please. Please. Isn't it best for everybody?

CARRIE. I don't know about everybody. I'm not used to thinking that way. I just think about what's best for us, for Julian.

LILY. That's what I want, too. What's best for Julian. Please tell me.

CARRIE. (*Carefully, as if anxious to impress the words.*) I don't know that I can. The people in the bank always talk of Mr. Warkins as a low-high-born man, tough and tricky, with plenty of riff-raff friends to do his dirty work. Julian isn't fit to deal with such a man and God knows what could happen. Warkins is not a man to joke with.

LILY. (*After the words "what will happen," LILY has picked up the phone and given the operator the number "LaFitte 1707." Her voice is firm.*) Tell Mr. Warkins that Lily Berniers, Lily Prine, must speak to him immediately and does not wish to be kept waiting. (*Waiting, she smiles at CARRIE.*) I think that's the way Mama would say it. Oh, hello, Mr. Cyrus, this is Lily. Mr. Cyrus, you mustn't blame anybody if I tell you something. Will you promise a sacred promise on the life of your child?

CARRIE. (*Above L. chair.*) He hasn't got a child.

LILY. But you haven't got a child. (*Pause.*) Then why did you make a sacred promise on a child you haven't got? You mustn't joke with me, Mr. Cyrus, you must not. Oh. I see. Well, please tell your wife I'm not mad a bit. That's first. Just ask her to give me one more year with Julian and I'll promise— Well, that's all. Just ask her that. (*She listens.*) I wouldn't like to say because I don't understand much myself. Why does it matter? I don't see why it should. Oh. Well, Miss Carrie heard— (*CARRIE wheels about.*) A *lady* heard Henry say it. Henry? Why, the Henry of my mother—you know. Just that once, a long time ago, Julian had been kind to your wife, and that maybe she was helping him now. I don't know how Henry knew. (*After a second.*) Oh, yes. I do. Henry is cousin to Mrs. Warkins. Yes, cousin. (*She *waits, looks puzzled.*) Mr. Cyrus? Mr. Cyrus? No, I don't think your wife's coming here. If she were, I could have asked her myself. I thought you could go right away, before she gets on the train— (*To* CARRIE.) He wants to know where he can find her to give her my message. (*Into phone.*) I don't know.

CARRIE. Something about Sailor's Lane near the depot.

LILY. Something about Sailor's Lane near the depot. Yes. Nobody's done anything bad, you understand, Mr. Cyrus, and tell her I know that, but I'd just like to ask to have Julian for one more— Mr. Cyrus? Well, thank you. (*She puts the phone down, sits, smiles.*) He says he sure will go talk to her. (*Crosses to screen door.*)

(CARRIE *sighs, sits* R. *chair.* ANNA *comes into the room, dressed in a suit. She looks at* LILY, *who does not notice her. She crosses to the table, leaves the boat ticket.*)

ANNA. We can't go together now. What would you like to do about these boat tickets?

CARRIE. We can't go together *now*? I don't know what you mean. Were we ever going?

ANNA. I thought so. When Julian brought these home to us, he thought so.

CARRIE. How strange you are. Did Julian think that? I suppose so; one piece of nonsense makes for ten. We never in our lives had any intention of going, you know that as well as I do.

(ANNA *picks up two valises and exits with them, placing them on porch.*)

LILY. (*Crosses to* R. *of* CARRIE.) I did right, just exactly. Didn't I? And I'll take the knife of truth and swear to keep my word—

CARRIE. Yes. But would you do it some place else? It would be nice to see you in a dress. Why don't you try it?

LILY. Oh. All right.

(*She exits* U. C. CARRIE *sits down, as if exhausted.* ANNA
comes back into the room.)

ANNA. (*At door.*) You never wanted to go to Europe?
Never meant to go?

CARRIE. How do you know such things? You go on
talking the way you always talked, saying you like or
want what you always said. (ANNA *doesn't answer. She
begins to recite in a make-fun sing-song.* ANNA *crosses
to* L.)

> "On the fairest time of June
> You may go, with sun or moon,
> Or the seven stars to light you
> Or the polar ray to right you,"

Do you still like it, all the nights you read it to us?

ANNA. Yes. (*Slowly.*) I don't know. I suppose it
doesn't mean much to me any more.

CARRIE. I can hear you, all your cultured evenings.
(*Recites.*) "To see the laurel wreath on high suspended,
That is to crown our name when life is ended."

ANNA. (*Standing near the piano, she plays a few
chords.*) And you this? So deeply felt, your favorite.

CARRIE. Was it?

ANNA. (*Smiles.*) And the candied oranges I brought
each week?

CARRIE. (*Rises and puts phone book back in stand.*)
I was sick of them ten years ago.

ANNA. (*Softly.*) Well, people change and forget to
tell each other. Too bad—causes so many mistakes. (*She
crosses to table, takes a ship's ticket from the envelope,
puts the envelope back on the table.*) I've taken my
ticket, left yours in the envelope. You'll explain about
that to Julian.

CARRIE. What are you talking about?

ANNA. (*Crosses to valise below piano.*) I'll spend the
night at the hotel. I'm going to Europe tomorrow

CARRIE. (*Moves toward her, stares at her, starts to
laugh.*) You will be lonely.

ANNA. That's all right. I always have been.

CARRIE. You will look very silly, a middle-aged,

scared-to-death woman, all by herself, trying to have a good time.

ANNA. (*Crosses* C. *with bag.*) You will stay here until you sell the house?

CARRIE. I don't believe you mean to go anywhere. It's just too crazy. You've never been any place in your life.

ANNA. (*Moves toward door.*) We have said good-bye.

CARRIE. (*Blocks her way.*) You're showing off. You're just plain showing off. You're not going anywhere— (*As* ANNA *reaches the door.*) You can't go before Julian. It would kill him to know that anything was wrong between us.

ANNA. You don't love me, but you want me to stay with you.

CARRIE. We will find a way to live.

ANNA. No. (*Crosses to porch, puts bag down.*)

CARRIE. (*Through window.*) You need me. You always have. Julian, everybody, always thought you the strong and sturdy—

ANNA. And you the frail, the flutter, the soft. That's the way you wanted them to think. I knew better. Our patched-together supper, a little talk, sometimes a book, "Long Ago" on the piano, a game of casino, your bath, then mine, your room and my room, two doors closed.

CARRIE. All those years of nights, all the things you knew and never said. Does everybody live like that, or just two old maids?

ANNA. I loved you and so whatever I knew didn't matter. You wanted to see yourself a way you never were. Maybe that's a game you let people play when you love them. Well, we had made something together, and the words would have stayed where they belonged as we waited for our brother to need us again. But our brother doesn't need us any more, and so the poor house came down. (*Crosses down steps.*)

CARRIE. (*Crossing to porch.*) I think our brother will need us. Now or some day. And we must stay together for it. (*Softly.*) You're the kind of woman with no place to go, no place to go. (*Smiles.*) You see? Some of those nights I thought about you, too. We must find a way to live.

ANNA. I don't wish to find a way to live with you. I am a woman who has no place to go, but I am going, and after a while I will ask myself why I took my mother's two children to be my own.

CARRIE. Unpack your bags.

ANNA. (*With great force.*) Pretend it's last week. You've just told the girls in the bank that you can't have coffee, you have to hurry home, that Anna will be mad at you for being late, that Anna gives the orders to the soft and tender you. Go back and pretend it's still last week. (CARRIE *retreats to parlor, exits* U. L. ANNA *pauses, then crosses and picks up camellia plant* L. *at steps.* MRS. PRINE *appears.* HENRY *is with her, but he waits beyond the garden fence.*) Will I look very foolish carrying a camellia plant to Europe?

ALBERTINE. I don't think so. It's most becoming. Soft around the face.

(ANNA *crosses* U. R. *in yard.* LILY *appears. She is dressed, has on her hat, is neat and cheerful.*)

LILY. (*On porch. To* ANNA.) Are you coming to New York with us? I would like that, Miss Anna.

ANNA. You shouldn't like it, and I'm not coming with you. (*She moves around the side of the house, gets camellia from urn.*) I guess two plants ain't more foolish than one. (*Exits* U. R.)

LILY. (*Crosses to* ALBERTINE *at* C. *in yard.*) Good-bye, Mama. We're going away. Good-bye. (*Smiles.*) I know that will make you happy.

ALBERTINE. Here's your ring, Lily.

LILY. Oh. Thank you. I had forgotten— Oh. Madame Celeste gave it to you?

ALBERTINE. Madame Celeste sold it to me. (*Very sharply.*) Sit down. (LILY *sits down on* L. *seat;* ALBERTINE *above* R. *of her, speaks very quietly, but as if the words had been rehearsed.*) I've had enough of whatever you're doing. However innocent is your innocence, I've had enough. More important, it is leading you into dangerous alleys. Not even for you will I again spend time in what you call an upstairs room with a morphine addict who holds seances to cover up what she sells.

LILY. (*In a fury, crosses to* R., *then* C. *to her* MOTHER.) I don't believe you, I don't believe you, I don't believe you. You want to take my friend from me—

ALBERTINE. (L. *of her.*) I am tired. I am sad. It is not good to know that my child swore fidelity to such a woman, and gave her wedding ring as proof.

LILY. My friend is a sweet friend. I gave her my ring because she loved me and gave me courage—

ALBERTINE. You are a pure girl and I believe you. (*Seats her on table.*) Now listen: I am going to give you a good-bye present. Try to make use of it: the pure and the innocent sometimes bring harm to themselves and those they love and, when they do, for some reason that I do not know, the injury is very great.

LILY. (*Who hasn't heard a word.*) You have talked this way about my friend because you want to bring me pain. Henry makes plans to pain me— (*Outside the fence,* HENRY *turns, enters yard.*) As you lie in bed with him, Henry makes the plans and tells you what to do.

ALBERTINE. (*Pleasantly, turns toward* HENRY.) Is that what we do in bed? (*To* LILY.) You think that's what we do in bed? You're wrong. It's where I forget the mistakes I made with you.

HENRY. (*Above bench.*) Stop it.

ALBERTINE. (*Ignores him; as if she were out of his control.*) If something is the matter with you, come home and I will care for you, as I should, as I should. But if nothing is the matter with you, have pity and leave me alone. I tried with you all your life, but I did not do well, and for that I ask your pardon. But don't punish me forever, Lily.

LILY. (*Softly.*) Is something the matter with me, Mama?

ALBERTINE. (*Very gently.*) No, darling. Certainly not.

LILY. If Julian leaves me—

ALBERTINE. Julian loves you, Lily.

LILY. I have sent a message and will keep my word. If Mrs. Warkins will give me one year—

ALBERTINE. (*After a second.*) You sent a message to Mrs. Warkins? Why?

LILY. Oh, because. I spoke to Mr. Warkins and told him to ask her to wait for Julian for one more year. (ALBERTINE *moves forward.* HENRY *moves toward her.* ALBERTINE *turns and stares at* HENRY.) After that, if Julian doesn't want me— Where would I ever go, who would ever want me? I'm trouble, we all know that. I wouldn't have anywhere to go.

ALBERTINE. (*After a long pause.*) You will come home to me. You are my child.

LILY. (*Warmly, sweetly.*) Thank you, Mama. Nice of you. But I couldn't go home to you—any more, as long as—

HENRY. If it ever happens, I won't be there. I won't be there.

LILY. Oh, thank you, Henry. That will be fine.

(JULIAN *appears, stumbling toward the house. His face and hands are cut and bruised. He has been beaten, and one leg is injured. He moves toward the garden in great pain; his face is so stern that the people who see him know that to assist him would be to undignify him.* LILY *makes a loud sound.* JULIAN *clings to pillar of the porch.* HENRY *goes toward* JULIAN, *but* JULIAN *puts up a hand, and* HENRY *halts.* ALBERTINE *crosses to porch.* CARRIE *enters parlor from* U. L. *Holds* U. L. *in horror.*)

JULIAN. I took Charlotte to her brother's house. She'll be all right, but not her face. She's safe there, I think— Do you know what Charlotte I'm talking about?

HENRY. Yes.

JULIAN. She'd better not stay where she is. Just in case. Not in this town.

HENRY. All right.

(*Painfully, slowly,* JULIAN *moves up steps. He slips.* HENRY *catches him and helps him through door.* ALBERTINE *holds it open.* ANNA *dashes from* U. C. R. *to kitchen* D. L.)

CARRIE. (*Softly, moving toward him.*) Doctor?

JULIAN. (*Clings to C. table.*) No. My friend. My poor friend. All she wanted, saved for, thought about— (*He gasps as if he were sick.*) to get away forever. Standing there, standing in the alley, they slashed us up.

ALBERTINE. (*Crosses in to R. of him.*) Who?

JULIAN. I don't know who. I saw two men and then I didn't see anything else. Two thugs he sent—

ALBERTINE. Who sent?

JULIAN. (*In a shout.*) Mr. Cyrus Warkins sent his men to meet us. Nobody knew she came to Chicago to tell me, nobody knew she put up the money for the land, nobody knew her name. Tell her I swear it, I swear it. (*To* ANNA *who comes toward him from kitchen with basin and wash cloth.*) Go away. (*She puts basin on piano stool. To* HENRY.) I told nobody. Tell her I swear it on my life—

HENRY. (R. *of him.*) No need to tell her that.

JULIAN. But somebody did know. Somebody told him. My friend—wanted to help me, took a dangerous chance and did— (*Softly.*) You should see her. You should see her. Make her know I never spoke her name.

ALBERTINE. She will not think you did. I am certain she will not think you did.

JULIAN. (*He takes the crumpled money envelope from his coat pocket where it has been arranged as if it were a handkerchief, and throws it to the floor.*) That's what's left of the money.

ALBERTINE. Shall I go to the police for you, Julian?

JULIAN. I went. High up to Drummond.

ALBERTINE. Then perhaps—

JULIAN. No. I don't know what the thugs looked like— No matter what I said, I could see Drummond saying to himself that I made it up, never could have had fifty dollars in my pocket, not less a hundred and fifty thousand— (*Sits front edge of table.*)

ALBERTINE. I will go to Warkins. (*Crossing to porch.*)

JULIAN. What for? Is he going to tell you who told him, who he hired to beat us up— What for?

ALBERTINE. (*Stops, stares at* LILY, *seated bench in*

78

yard. HENRY *comes to porch.* ANNA *moves to screen door.*) I don't know.

JULIAN. Christ, what a mess-ass I am. She handed me the whole deal, told me every move to make, a baby could have done it.

LILY. Mama, I did it.

ALBERTINE. (*Crosses to her.*) Are you very sure you love him?

LILY. Mama, I did it. God forgive me.

ALBERTINE. Go in and sit by him. Just sit by him and shut up. Can you do that? Can you have enough pity for him not to kill him with the truth? Can you love him enough to go by him, sit down, (*Very softly, with great violence.*) *and be still?* (LILY *nods.*) Then go and do it. (LILY *moves into the house and timidly approaches* JULIAN. ALBERTINE *sinks down on bench.* HENRY *crosses to her.*)

JULIAN. (*Leans forward to touch* LILY's *hair.*) I don't look nice. Take off your hat, baby. We ain't going nowhere. There ain't nothing to go with.

LILY. May I wash your face? (*Sinks to her knees beside him.*)

JULIAN. (*Comforts her.*) Don't look like that. I'm all right. Nobody ever beat me up before, or slashed a friend.

CARRIE. (*Crosses* D. L.) Things can happen.

JULIAN. What did you say?

CARRIE. I said bad things happen to people. Doesn't mean anything.

JULIAN. I mean the way you said it. Say it that way again.

CARRIE. (*Crosses toward him.*) I don't know what you mean. Why don't you go rest yourself, darling? Good hot bath—

JULIAN. (*Turns to stare at her.*) Why you start to purr at me? As if I'd done something good— (*Moves toward her.*) You're smiling. What the hell's there to smile at? You *like* me this way? (*After a second, rises to stare at the room.*) Pretty, all this. And the mortgage, and the tickets to Europe, and all the fun to come. **Pretty, wasn't it?**

CARRIE. (*Crosses U. C. toward* ANNA.) We didn't want them. (*To* ANNA.) Did we?

ANNA. No, we didn't want them. (*Crosses, gets bags from porch and exits U. L.*)

JULIAN. (*Sits L. chair. Gets wash cloth.*) Don't talk that way. Won't do me any good. Assing it up all my God damned life, all my life it's been the same. (*With violence.*) Nobody ever beat me up before. Nobody's ever going to beat me up again. (*There is a pause.* CARRIE *sighs and moves to porch door. Then, as if a decision has been made, she moves out to the porch and leans down to pick up the final piece of* ANNA's *luggage.*)

ALBERTINE. (*Very sharply to* CARRIE.) Mean to see a man stoke his pride. The meanest sight in the world. Don't you think?

CARRIE. (*Turns to look at her.*) Let's be glad nothing worse happened. We're together, the three of us, that's all that matters.

ALBERTINE. I counted four.

CARRIE. I mean the four of us.

ALBERTINE. Some day you will tell him about Lily? Then there will be three of you. Before you tell him, let me know. I will want to come for her.

CARRIE. (*Points inside.*) All that stuff has to go back, and the debts, got to find ourselves jobs. So much to do. (CARRIE *moves into the room, puts valise below door.*)

JULIAN. (*Cleaning face with wash cloth.*) Old saying, money is a real pure lady and when the world began she swore herself an oath never to belong to a man who didn't love her. I never loved her and she guessed it. Couldn't fool her, she got good sense. (*Softly, desperately.*) Nobody ever beat me up before. Maybe once it starts—

CARRIE. (*Crosses C.*) There's bad luck and then there's good luck. That's all.

JULIAN. I guess so. Well, I've had the bad. Maybe I got a little good luck coming to me. Other men make it easy. Plenty of room in this world for everybody. Just got to fight for it. Got to start again, start again. (*He starts to rise.*)

CARRIE. (*Gets purse from U. R. sideboard.*) I'm going

to get something nice to make soup with. You always liked a good soup when you didn't feel well. Meat and marrow, the way you like it. (*As she gets to porch door.*) Tomorrow's another day. (*Stops on porch before she moves past* HENRY *and* ALBERTINE *in the garden.*) Goodbye, Mrs. Prine. (*She exits. After a second* HENRY *puts his hand on* ALBERTINE'S *shoulder.*)

HENRY. Good-bye. (*He exits. In the room* JULIAN *is moving painfully toward his bedroom.* LILY, *timidly holding back, joins him. He leans on her as they move out together.* ANNA *crosses to pick up her bag and, at the same time,* ALBERTINE *rises to exit.*)

CURTAIN

TOYS IN THE ATTIC

PROPERTY PLOT

Prop Table Right:
Ice tub with ice pick and burlap cover
½ bushel basket (peat moss) with burlap cover
Banjo case
Large brown suitcase (JULIAN)
Small black suitcase (LILY)
Wicker basket with handle (champagne)
Double-depth dress box (blue-grey flowered):
   (Packing order, bottom up)
   Tissue
   Brown evening cape, black fur collar
   Tissue
   Red evening cape, mink collar trim
   Tissue
   Black sequined evening dress
   Tissue
   Green evening dress
   Tissue
Dress box (pink with roses):
   (Packing order, bottom up)
   Tissue
   Anna's hat, garnet bracelet in purple case, gold mesh bag
      with boat tickets in envelope
   Tissue
   Red negligee
   Tissue
Dress box (yellow with flowers):
   Tissue
   Fur piece
   Tissue
Hat box:
   Tissue
   Red hat with poppies
   Tissue
2 glove boxes:
   Tissue wrapped elbow-length evening gloves in each
2 dummy dress boxes with decorative ribbon, tied with heavy
      gold cord
Julian's raincoat
The box unit carried in by the taxi-driver is made by stacking
      box of furs on bottom, double-depth box on fur box. Hat
      box and glove boxes are on top of double depth box.
      Raincoat is draped over this stack to help conceal they
      are gift boxes

Gold wedding band, check, chauffeur's cap, crumpled money
    envelope, car door slam, roll of money
Prop table left:
Oval tray:
    Serving bowl with shrimp and serving spoon
    Serving bowl with rice and serving spoon
Tray:
    Opened bottle of champagne
    4 tumblers, ¼ full champagne
    1 dish with crackers
    1 opened can caviar with teaspoon
Breakfast tray:
    Dinner dish, covered with napkin
    Cup and saucer
    Knife, fork and spoon
    Napkin
Card table
Glass of orange juice
Peroxide bottle with gauze pad
Coffee pot with coffee
Coffee cup and saucer
Broom—white wash-basin with water and face cloth
Shirt cardboard
Pitcher of ice tea
Small bowl of cracked ice
Mantilla in flowered gift box
Three suitcases, large, medium, small (ANNA)
Packing clothes (used in Act Two):
    1 grey suit on left parlor chair
    1 rust suit on spinet
    1 grey dress on spinet
    1 navy dress offstage L-2
    1 figured dress offstage L-2
    1 blue knit dress offstage L-1
    2 pairs shoes, flats, pumps (ANNA)

Prop Set Up Center:
Spinet and bench
Refrigerator
Knife of truth
Julian's shirt (Act Two)
Julian's coat and tie (Act Three)
Banjo (Act Three)

Preset Yard Act One:
R.—bench, L.—stool, C.—table, trash basket to marks
Hose
Mint
High urn
(Act Two and Three) Furniture to marks

Preset Porch Act One:
Rocker
Carryall:
  Palm fan, cologne in gift wrap, Kleenex
Carrie's hand bag with mirror, comb, lipstick, gloves
Fern stand
Sprinkling can (small) with water
Table with three plants:
  Camellia, violets, geranium
Newspaper under plant table

Preset Parlor Act One:
Piano with music book open on it
Doilie and bowl of flowers on c. table
c.—table to marks
R.—chair to marks
L.—chair to marks
Piano stool at piano
R.—stool front of R. chair
Telephone table with stand telephone and telephone book under
Window seat bench
Table at window for plants, pot of ivy, pot of geraniums
Duplicate diamond ring to Mark
Sideboard—U. R.: two knives, forks, spoons, three place mats,
       two napkins, salt and peppers, dressing, books. dishes,
       photos, travel folders, etc.
Sideboard—U. L.:
  Two dinner dishes
  Ice tea glasses (three)
  Scissors
  Anna's purse with bank-book
  Tabasco sauce
  Serving bowl for rice (double of rice bowl off L.)
  Dressing, books. platters, bric-a-brac, tea cups and saucers
       on stands

Strike at End of Act One:
Champagne tray, glasses, tea glasses, banjo, mortgage, carryall,
       tickets, Anna's bag, gift clothes, spinet bench, song book

Parlor Preset Act Two:
Refrigerator to marks
Spinet to marks
Clothes on spinet and L. chair
Close piano key cover
Piano stool to D. L. marks
Anna's large bag, shoe polish, rag and tissue L. of L. chair
Carrie's gloves on window table—Carrie's purse U. L.
Gift dress boxes stacked on piano
Box with mantilla on piano

Four flower pots on window table:
    Two camellias, one ivy, one geranium
Palm fan on R. sideboard
Tickets in envelope to offstage piano L-2

Strike After Act Two:
Coffee pot and cup
Orange juice
Peroxide bottle

Parlor Preset Act Three:
Spinet to marks
Piano stool to marks
Anna's medium case to below piano with large case
Open piano
Carrie's bag and fan on U. R. sideboard

Personal Props:
JULIAN: Wrist watch, envelope with $150,000, mortgage, diamond ring in ring box, pocket money, shaving cream, bloody handkerchief
CARRIE: Wrist watch, topaz pin
ALBERTINE: Parasol
LILY: Gold wedding band

COSTUME LIST

CARRIE BERNIERS:
 Sage green dress (with print piping on collar and sleeves)
 Tan shantung dress (lace at neck and sleeves)
 Beige bag
 Rust shoes

ANNA BERNIERS:
 Medium blue shantung dress
 Plum colored wrap-around apron
 Sage green dress and jacket
 Black shoes
 Brown shoes
 Black straw hat
 Brown bag
 Gloves

ALBERTINE PRINE:
 Blue and white silk print dress and coat
 Orchid voile dress
 Silk slip
 Horse hair hat
 Beige gloves
 Beige shoes
 Green shoes
 Beige parasol
 Gray bag
 Beads

LILY BERNIERS:
 Pink linen dress and jacket
 Pink tam
 Yellow shantung dress
 Beige felt tam
 White nylon robe
 Pink half-slip
 Blue silk slip
 Beige felt hat
 Gray kid gloves
 Yellow linen shoes
 Beige tweed coat (yellow lined)

JULIAN BERNIERS:
 Gray-blue Glen plaid suit
 Black straw moccasins
 Beige shirt
 Dark gray tie

Black socks
Tan worsted suit (with duplicate—beat up)
Blue shirt (with duplicate—beat up)
Light gray tie (with duplicate—beat up)
Blue patterned silk dressing gown

GUS:
Beige work pants
Sneakers
Tan shirt
Leather shoulder to knee apron

HENRY SIMPSON:
Pale blue washable summer suit
Blue shirt
Dark tie
Black shoes
Black socks

TAXI DRIVER:
Battered panama hat
Light tan striped flannel pants (belt and suspenders)
Light tan shirt
Tan vest
Black and white shoes

FIRST DELIVERY MAN:
White linen cap
Blue shirt
Light gray work pants (suspenders)
Black work shoes

SECOND DELIVERY MAN:
Old panama hat
Maroon shirt
Tan work pants
G.I. work shoes
Shoulder to knee work apron

THIRD DELIVERY MAN:
Straw visor cap
Dark blue and green checked cotton shirt
Gray work pants (belt)
Gray vest
G.I. work shoes

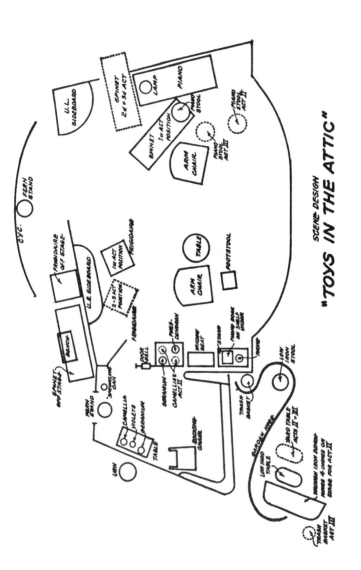

SCENE DESIGN

"TOYS IN THE ATTIC"

French Lesson*

(Trop Cheres: CARRIE)

MARC BLITZSTEIN

Andante

Un - e cham - bre pour deux dam - es. Have you one room for two

lad - ies? Ah non! Trop chè - res! Oh no! Too ex -

pen -sive! Mer - ci, mais au re - voir. Trop chè - res. Too ex -

pen - sive. Mer - ci m' - sieur. Trop chè - res.

Big Day

(Julian)

MARC BLITZSTEIN

sis - ter and for broth - er, going to be a Bern - ier

G   G   G   D7

day.   And for Ma - ma and for Pa - pa and for

G   G   D7

p

sis - ter and for broth-er, going to be just a Bern - ier day._____

G   G   D7   G   G

ff

NEW PLAYS

★ **AT HOME AT THE ZOO by Edward Albee.** Edward Albee delves deeper into his play THE ZOO STORY by adding a first act, HOMELIFE, which precedes Peter's fateful meeting with Jerry on a park bench in Central Park. "An essential and heartening experience." *–NY Times.* "Darkly comic and thrilling." *–Time Out.* "Genuinely fascinating." *–Journal News.* [2M, 1W] ISBN: 978-0-8222-2317-7

★ **PASSING STRANGE book and lyrics by Stew, music by Stew and Heidi Rodewald, created in collaboration with Annie Dorsen.** A daring musical about a young bohemian that takes you from black middle-class America to Amsterdam, Berlin and beyond on a journey towards personal and artistic authenticity. "Fresh, exuberant, bracingly inventive, bitingly funny, and full of heart." *–NY Times.* "The freshest musical in town!" *–Wall Street Journal.* "Excellent songs and a vulnerable heart." *–Variety.* [4M, 3W] ISBN: 978-0-8222-2400-6

★ **REASONS TO BE PRETTY by Neil LaBute.** Greg really, truly adores his girlfriend, Steph. Unfortunately, he also thinks she has a few physical imperfections, and when he mentions them, all hell breaks loose. "Tight, tense and emotionally true." *–Time Magazine.* "Lively and compulsively watchable." *–The Record.* [2M, 2W] ISBN: 978-0-8222-2394-8

★ **OPUS by Michael Hollinger.** With only a few days to rehearse a grueling Beethoven masterpiece, a world-class string quartet struggles to prepare their highest-profile performance ever—a televised ceremony at the White House. "Intimate, intense and profoundly moving." *–Time Out.* "Worthy of scores of bravissimos." *–BroadwayWorld.com.* [4M, 1W] ISBN: 978-0-8222-2363-4

★ **BECKY SHAW by Gina Gionfriddo.** When an evening calculated to bring happiness takes a dark turn, crisis and comedy ensue in this wickedly funny play that asks what we owe the people we love and the strangers who land on our doorstep. "As engrossing as it is ferociously funny." *–NY Times.* "Gionfriddo is some kind of genius." *–Variety.* [2M, 3W] ISBN: 978-0-8222-2402-0

★ **KICKING A DEAD HORSE by Sam Shepard.** Hobart Struther's horse has just dropped dead. In an eighty-minute monologue, he discusses what path brought him here in the first place, the fate of his marriage, his career, politics and eventually the nature of the universe. "Deeply instinctual and intuitive." *–NY Times.* "The brilliance is in the infinite reverberations Shepard extracts from his simple metaphor." *–TheaterMania.* [1M, 1W] ISBN: 978-0-8222-2336-8

DRAMATISTS PLAY SERVICE, INC.
440 Park Avenue South, New York, NY 10016 212-683-8960 Fax 212-213-1539
postmaster@dramatists.com www.dramatists.com

NEW PLAYS

★ **AUGUST: OSAGE COUNTY by Tracy Letts.** WINNER OF THE 2008 PULITZER PRIZE AND TONY AWARD. When the large Weston family reunites after Dad disappears, their Oklahoma homestead explodes in a maelstrom of repressed truths and unsettling secrets. "Fiercely funny and bitingly sad." –*NY Times.* "Ferociously entertaining." –*Variety.* "A hugely ambitious, highly combustible saga." –*NY Daily News.* [6M, 7W] ISBN: 978-0-8222-2300-9

★ **RUINED by Lynn Nottage.** WINNER OF THE 2009 PULITZER PRIZE. Set in a small mining town in Democratic Republic of Congo, RUINED is a haunting, probing work about the resilience of the human spirit during times of war. "A full-immersion drama of shocking complexity and moral ambiguity." –*Variety.* "Sincere, passionate, courageous." –*Chicago Tribune.* [8M, 4W] ISBN: 978-0-8222-2390-0

★ **GOD OF CARNAGE by Yasmina Reza, translated by Christopher Hampton.** WINNER OF THE 2009 TONY AWARD. A playground altercation between boys brings together their Brooklyn parents, leaving the couples in tatters as the rum flows and tensions explode. "Satisfyingly primitive entertainment." –*NY Times.* "Elegant, acerbic, entertainingly fueled on pure bile." –*Variety.* [2M, 2W] ISBN: 978-0-8222-2399-3

★ **THE SEAFARER by Conor McPherson.** Sharky has returned to Dublin to look after his irascible, aging brother. Old drinking buddies Ivan and Nicky are holed up at the house too, hoping to play some cards. But with the arrival of a stranger from the distant past, the stakes are raised ever higher. "Dark and enthralling Christmas fable." –*NY Times.* "A timeless classic." –*Hollywood Reporter.* [5M] ISBN: 978-0-8222-2284-2

★ **THE NEW CENTURY by Paul Rudnick.** When the playwright is Paul Rudnick, expectations are geared for a play both hilarious and smart, and this provocative and outrageous comedy is no exception. "The one-liners fly like rockets." –*NY Times.* "The funniest playwright around." –*Journal News.* [2M, 3W] ISBN: 978-0-8222-2315-3

★ **SHIPWRECKED! AN ENTERTAINMENT—THE AMAZING ADVENTURES OF LOUIS DE ROUGEMONT (AS TOLD BY HIMSELF) by Donald Margulies.** The amazing story of bravery, survival and celebrity that left nineteenth-century England spellbound. Dare to be whisked away. "A deft, literate narrative." –*LA Times.* "Springs to life like a theatrical pop-up book." –*NY Times.* [2M, 1W] ISBN: 978-0-8222-2341-2

DRAMATISTS PLAY SERVICE, INC.
440 Park Avenue South, New York, NY 10016 212-683-8960 Fax 212-213-1539
postmaster@dramatists.com www.dramatists.com